Stowers, Carlton.

Where dreams die
hard.

$22.95

DATE			

WHERE DREAMS
DIE HARD

WHERE DREAMS DIE HARD

A SMALL AMERICAN TOWN AND ITS SIX-MAN FOOTBALL TEAM

CARLTON STOWERS

DA CAPO PRESS
A Member of the Perseus Books Group

Portions of this book originally appeared in *Parade* magazine, the *Houston Chronicle*, and the *Dallas Observer*, though in slightly different form.

Designed by Jeff Williams
Set in 12-point Fairfield Light by the Perseus Books Group

Library of Congress Cataloging-in-Publication Data

Stowers, Carlton.
    Where dreams die hard : a small American town and its six-man football team /
Carlton Stowers.—1st Da Capo Press ed.
        p. cm.
    ISBN-10: 0-306-81404-8 (hardcover : alk. paper)
    ISBN-13: 978-0-306-81404-4 (hardcover : alk. paper)
    1. Penelope High School (Penelope, Tex.) 2. Football—Social aspects—Texas—
Penelope. 3. Penelope (Tex.)—Social life and customs—21st century. I. Title.

GV958.P42S86 2005
796.332'62'09764283—DC22

                                                                                    2005006983

First Da Capo Press edition 2005

Published by Da Capo Press
A Member of the Perseus Books Group
www.dacapopress.com

Da Capo Press books are available at special discounts for bulk purchases in the U.S. by corporations, institutions, and other organizations. For more information, please contact the Special Markets Department at the Perseus Books Group, 11 Cambridge Center, Cambridge, MA 02142, or call (800) 255-1514 or (617) 252-5298, or e-mail special.markets@perseusbooks.com.

1 2 3 4 5 6 7 8 9—09 08 07 06 05

To

IRA MILTON STOWERS

1918–2004

*How I would love to sit
and talk football with you
just one more time*

"Six-man football? Ain't that a ranch kids' game?"

"Ranch kids are tough. In six-man ball you've got no place to hide. It's run-and-gun. It takes smarts. And one last thing: There's the slaughter rule. Any time a team gets ahead of you by 45 points, it's the end of the game. I've never been slaughter ruled and I intend to keep it that way . . . "

—THE SLAUGHTER RULE

"Just where in the hell is Penelope, Texas?"

"It's east of West."

—COFFEE SHOP CONVERSATION

CONTENTS

ACKNOWLEDGMENTS

For keeping me abreast of things transpiring elsewhere in the high school football world during the time the Penelope story was being played out, I thank the *Dallas Morning News, Waco Tribune Herald,* and sixmanfootball.com. *King Football: Greatest Moments in Texas High School Football History* provided insight into Willie Nelson's days as an Abbott High Panther. Tim Sweeten's documentary film "The Seventh Man" was an inspiration. As was Laura Wilson's *Grit and Glory,* a superlative photo essay on the six-man game.

I would be remiss—and likely denied meals and clean shirts—if I did not say special thanks to Pat Stowers, my wife and favorite photographer. And I'll forever be grateful to literary agent Jim Donovan and Da Capo Press editor Kevin Hanover for embracing the idea of this little book.

Most important, of course, were the people who let me into their homes, their hearts, their locker rooms, and their community. You're about to read all their names, so I'll not mention them again for fear of overlooking someone. To each and all, my sincere thanks.

PREFACE

In those dark and troubling days that followed the events of 9/11, I was among the many who fell into catatonic disbelief of the vicious anger, the blatant evil that had visited my homeland. For days I did little but stare blankly into the television screen, watching as images of destruction and death were pounded repeatedly into the American consciousness.

And as I did so I weighed a heavy decision.

As a journalist, I had walked among the ruins of the terrorist-bombed Murrah Federal Building in Oklahoma City, watched as flames engulfed Branch Davidian leader David Koresh and his followers just outside Waco, seen the ravages of killer tornadoes, and written too many books and articles about man's inhumanity to man. Haunting though such memories were, they paled in comparison to the vision of thousands dying as the Twin Towers crumbled into an ominous boiling cloud of dust and debris. That far distant event, in a manner of speaking, became a benchmark moment in my career as a writer.

In time the depression that swept over me became frightening, growing into numbing concern with what I came to perceive as a hurricane of ills that threatened the well-being I'd so willingly come to accept during my adult life. Too much crime and corruption, too many dangerous dark alleys where evil never slept, a growing decline of patience and tolerance, and now the murderous attack from an enemy previously invisible to me. I had, I finally came to realize, reached a point of absolute overdose on the dark side. Always a rich harvesting ground of journalism, murder and mayhem, political bomb-throwing, war, drugs, racial unrest, and corporate corruption had long provided more than ample headline fodder. And suddenly I wanted no more of it.

When a young editor argued that what those of us under her charge had to provide readers was more "red meat," more hard-hitting, finger-pointing controversy, I rolled my eyes and began considering my leave-taking. Though fully aware that there were endless fakes and frauds needing exposure and countless crimes begging courthouse justice, such tasks no longer interested me. It was time to let someone else try to sort reason from the unreasonable, spend days in the company of devastated victims, and chronicle the social ills for which there seemed no cure.

Thus I began a desperate search for a subject that would direct me back to some degree of comfort and innocence. I needed a sign that there were places where friendships did not end over blue state–red state political views, where illogical blame-placing had replaced initiative, where crime statistics didn't continue to rise and suffocate neighborhoods. Where "red meat" was not the literary special of the day.

Term it cowardly retreat if you like, but I was determined to seek out a quieter locale from which to tell my stories.

On a warm, golden evening that belied my mood, I drove to the home of my five-year-old granddaughter and suggested an adventure. An hour's drive away, in the picturesque lakeside community of Granbury, Texas, the Brazos Drive-In, one of the few outdoor movie theaters still in operation in the state, was showing a G-rated picture. It was time, I explained to her mother, for young McLean to experience the unique pleasure I had known as a child growing up in rural West Texas. I stopped short of admission that I was in retreat to a simpler place and time, with far less hate and destruction and worry for the future. Instead, I talked only of watching a movie under the stars, of hot popcorn and icy sodas in the concession stand, of youngsters running free on the playground at the base of the screen.

McLean, carefree and oblivious of my concerns for the world she was fast growing into, quickly set about getting ready to go.

I cannot tell you the plot of the movie shown that evening. Instead of watching the screen, I focused on my granddaughter's delight as she drank in the new and wondrous sights and sounds, giggling at something funny on the screen, meeting other children brought by parents no doubt there for the same reason I had come. Her joy gently pushed my own pessimism aside, and for the first time in longer than I wished to remember, I felt new hope and faith and optimism—calling out to me from the voice of a child.

That night, as we made our way home, McLean sleeping peacefully beside me, I knew too soon there would come a time when she and those of her generation would be called on to confront the ills and evils of an imperfect world. And it was important that I do what I could to assure her she would also find warmth and goodness, strength and resolve. And love.

Thus began my quest to find that quiet, restorative world inhabited by those who call the American heartland home. And I discovered it not far away, in a small town just an hour's drive south of Dallas; a place where its residents feel no need to lock their doors at night, where there is not so much as a single blinking red light slowing main street traffic, where only 211 people live, and where the entire town comes together every Friday night during the fall when its Penelope High Wolverines suit up and play the game of six-man football.

You'll find no "red meat" in this journal; only a simple tale of a remarkable place and its even more remarkable people.

1

THEY WERE VISIBLE ON THE FLATLAND HORIZON FROM MILES away, rural beacons signaling that the fall ritual of Texas high school football was again under way. Down Farm Road 308, past the sprawling cotton fields and sun-browned pastureland that dot the region, the stadium lights lured fans to the beginning of a new season filled with the eternal tradition of high hope and grand anticipation.

On this short-sleeve September evening in the tiny pickup-truck-and-baseball-cap hamlet of Penelope, where they play a strange and fast-paced game called six-man football, it was the social event of the week. Long before the kickoff, local farmers had begun to gather around the chain-link fence bordering the playing field to compare progress of their summer grain harvest and the well-being of their livestock, and to report recent readings from their rain gauges. Moms tended the already busy concession stand while energetic grade school children chose sides for pass-touch games to be played behind the stands.

On the field, the fourteen members of the Penelope High School Wolverines, proud in their bright red uniforms and white helmets, were earnestly going through pregame drills. And even though too many passes were dropped, too many punts failed to spiral, team speed was noticeable only by its absence, and they had already opened the season with back-to-back road defeats, the enthusiasm of those filing into the tiny stadium was palpable. It was the first home game of the year, an opportunity for most of the townspeople to personally judge the talent of the 2004 squad.

Earlier, the mesquite smoke aroma of burgers being grilled by players' dads in the parking lot had greeted those paying their three-dollar admission. There had been the traditional pregame "Meet the Wolverines" dinner in the nearby school cafeteria, accompanied by an announcement that student members of the Future Farmers of America would be raffling off chances for a variety of homemade cakes and pies.

The scene made it difficult to imagine that just four years earlier, the Penelope Independent School District, the sixteenth poorest in the state, had had neither a football team nor an inclination to field one. Forty years ago it had briefly given football a try for a few winless seasons be-

fore abandoning the sport, satisfied to limit its extracurricular activities to basketball, volleyball, a few spring sports,
and one-act play competitions.

As in so many back road communities forgotten in the
desperate rush to big-city promise and prosperity, the woe-
ful signals that Penelope was dying a slow, quiet death were
obvious.

Penelope was named after the daughter of a Great Northern
Railroad official who founded the town in 1902 as a watering
stop for passing steam engines. Longtime postmistress Mary
Dvorak remembers her mother telling stories of a thriving
little community that once included three grocery stores, a
couple of hotels, several churches, a lumberyard, a phar-
macy with a doctor's office upstairs, a feed and hardware
store, an ice house, three active cotton gins, and a railroad
depot.

In a tattered folder she keeps on hand as proof of better
days is a collection of faded photographs of Penelope as it
once was. Now, however, the local granary and her tiny
post office are the only businesses left. "Unless," she
smiles, "you count the soft drink machine over there in
front of the Volunteer Fire Department." Flanking the one-
room building from where she dispatches the mail is a sad
row of weathered and boarded-up buildings that run the
one-block length of what was once called "downtown."

Until a city limits sign suddenly appears on a rise, there is no warning to passing travelers that they're about to arrive in Penelope. No skyline, except for the granary's storage silo and the ghostly remains of a long-abandoned cotton gin. Were it not for a state historical society–sponsored marker that recalls more prosperous times, one would not know that one of its half dozen paintless, crumbling buildings had once been a thriving grocery. Or that just across the highway from a pen of frolicking goats a gas station once offered full service and soda pop for locals and passersby. Most who might remember the town's better days now reside in the well-kept cemetery located on a nearby hillside.

The residential part of town, meanwhile, is a random mixture that pleads a strong case for zoning regulations. A scattering of modern brick homes with neatly kept yards are neighbors to doublewide trailers or ancient frame houses in varying states of aging and disrepair. Rusted and retired farming equipment silently sits in weedy vacant lots. An occasional "Hay for Sale" sign is the only visible hint of local commerce.

Penelope is an antique badly in need of care and polish.

"There's no mystery to what happened here," Dvorak explains. "In 1960, the railroad shut down and cotton was no longer king." That devastating one-two punch sent shoppers and job seekers to nearby Hillsboro, Waco, and Dallas.

Today, with the exception of a small residential area inside the city limits, most of those whose mail she handles live in the countryside, earning meager profits while farming land that has been in the family for generations, sending their children off to school by bus every morning.

In town, the only paved streets are the intersecting farm roads that run through it.

Yet, as for many others, Penelope is Mary Dvorak's heartland. "It's a wonderful place to live," she says. "After I graduated from high school I moved up to Dallas for a couple of years. But I got enough of the big city real quick. I came home and I've never been sorry for a minute that I did. Like I've told my kids, I'm going to be here until they put me in that cemetery on the hill outside of town."

And, she adds, she'll continue to be a regular at the Wolverine football games. "We're proud of those young men. They may not be winning much, but they're giving their best, building something for the little ones down in junior high and elementary school."

Which is how school superintendent Harley Johnson views things. "Football was discontinued here in 1963," he explains, "and the idea of our ever playing again really never entered anyone's mind." Until in the spring of '99, when a junior student named Marvin Hill entered Johnson's office to say he'd been sent by several other underclassmen to ask if the school might again have a football team. "I told him to bring me a list of those who wanted to play. He brought me the names of fourteen students—juniors, sophomores, and freshmen—so I took the request to the school board."

The decision to add the sport came easily; putting the idea in motion didn't. "I don't think we even had a football, much less any uniforms and helmets," Johnson recalls. Nor did the school have a stadium in which to practice and play. Or anyone to coach the team.

The superintendent, a make-do kind of administrator used to stretching tight budgets and maximizing limited manpower, set about methodically resolving each problem: He persuaded members of the community to donate money needed for equipment and talked an old friend, retired from teaching and living in nearby Hubbard, into coaching the team. The difficulty posed by the absence of a football field was solved by holding practices on the school playground and a parking area adjacent to the nearby Catholic church. All of the games would be scheduled for the opposing teams' stadiums.

"Honestly," Johnson says, "my thinking was to wait and see if the kids would stick with it before we went to the expense and effort of building our own stadium." In fact, two Penelope seasons would pass before the school board voted to seek grant money and take out a sizable bank loan to purchase a two-acre pasture adjacent to the campus. With a great deal of volunteer help, they were soon building stands and fences, erecting lights and a scoreboard. A local farmer volunteered water from his stock tank to care for the newly planted grass. When Covington, a neighboring school south of Fort Worth, announced that it was advancing from the six-man ranks to play eleven-man ball, thus requiring the installation of regulation goalposts for its field, Johnson contacted the superintendent about the goalposts they were replacing. "Send somebody over here with a flatbed truck and some tie-down rope," the generous Covington school official had said, "and they're yours."

And, while the team had been winless in that first season, scoring only twenty points in its ten games, it was not without at least one moment of poetic irony. The first Penelope touchdown of the new era was scored by Hill, the youngster who had urged Johnson to reinstate the sport. In the second season came the school's first win.

And now, as the kickoff of the new year's first home game neared, it remained the school's only victory in four years. The two road losses that had launched this season had brought the modern-day Wolverines' won-lost record to an anemic 1 and 31.

Not that many in the football-crazed state had noticed. Six-man football is Texas's athletic stepchild, far beneath the radar that religiously monitors the Dallas Cowboys and Houston Texans, colleges major and minor, and eleven-man high school football wars. There are Saturday mornings when not so much as the score of the previous evening's Penelope game can be found in the major daily sports sections.

———

By rule, six-man football is reserved for the state's 112 public high schools with an enrollment of ninety-nine or fewer students. In hidden-away towns that test the geographical knowledge of even longtime Texans, they often play on fields poorly lighted and bare of grass, circled by trucks and cars filled with fans who view their weekly games through windows freshly cleaned down at Gus's Grocery and Gulf Station. A running back too small to earn even a second notice by coaches at larger schools scores a touchdown, and his heroic efforts are greeted by a mixture of cheers and honking horns. And it is not unusual, during the first weeks of each new season, for the sounds of shotgun blasts to echo from the nearby countryside during the games as local hunters busy themselves with the annual rites of dove season.

In the back road hamlets, where bleachers might accommodate one hundred to two hundred spectators, where there are rarely enough students to field a marching band to entertain at halftime, and where the team rosters rarely boast more than a dozen or so players, there is a strong argument to be made that rural America offers up the last outpost of organized sport played on shoestring budgets and simply for the joy of competition and camaraderie. No college scouts, in search of their next Heisman Trophy candidate, stop by. Among the youngsters who play the game, there are few unrealistic dreams of ever advancing to collegiate or professional stardom.

Yet the game goes on, Friday night after Friday night, year after year. Whereas school board members in Philadelphia, Pennsylvania, questioned the worth of athletics in Philadelphia's thirty-eight public schools a few years back and Los Angeles school officials were talking of discontinuing junior high football in the name of economics, Penelope fields a high school and junior high team on a bake sale budget that wouldn't even keep many of the state's large-enrollment athletic programs in jock straps and adhesive tape.

The sport they play began in the mid-1930s as the brainchild of a Chester, Nebraska, educator and coach named Stephen Epler, who recognized a void in the fall programs of small rural schools. Searching for a solution, he went to the drawing board and designed a game that would not require the customary eleven players. Football, he theorized, could be played with three linemen instead of seven, three backs instead of four.

In Epler's vision, the rules of the game would differ slightly. It would be played on an 80-yard field instead of the traditional 100; the offense would need to make 15 yards for a first down instead of the standard 10. Each quarter would last ten minutes instead of twelve, and all players, including the center, would be eligible to receive passes. And since it was unlikely that kicking specialists abounded in the Nebraska corn belt, he put a premium on such ability, ruling that following a touchdown, a kicked conversion would be worth two points and field goals four.

And aware that the talent levels of teams would vary greatly, he suggested a unique "mercy rule." If, at any point following halftime, one team was leading by forty-five points, the game would be ended.

As word of his new concept spread, so did interest. States throughout the Midwest adopted the hybrid sport, and in 1938, Rodney Kidd, then athletic director of the governing body of Texas high school athletics, wrote Epler for information.

Kidd then contacted coaches at two small Texas schools, Prairie Lea and Martindale, and asked that they study the rules, have their kids practice for a while, and then put on a spring exhibition game for him and other University Interscholastic League (UIL) officials.

They liked what they saw, and the following fall formerly non-football-playing schools in Dripping Springs, Harrold, and Oklaunion, as well as Prairie Lea and Martindale, were celebrating their first district championships.

The sport's popularity reached a national peak in 1953, when thirty-thousand rural schools across the country fielded teams. And while closings and consolidation of many small-town schools would ultimately turn six-man football into nothing more than scrapbook memories in many states, it has continued to thrive in Texas. Add a few schools still playing in Nebraska and isolated areas of New Mexico, Montana, Colorado, and Kansas, and the nationwide total of six-man-playing schools annually ranges between 225 and 250. And in Texas, it is no longer the sole property of country communities. The sudden growth of limited-enrollment urban private schools and the desire to provide the students with athletic opportunities has given rise to 75 new six-man teams in Texas alone.

I had searched without success to find more about the sport's origin and advancement. Epler had passed away years ago and I couldn't locate any additional information in libraries or on the Internet that offered any satisfactory historical enlightenment.

I resigned myself to knowing little about those pioneer days during which the foundation had been laid for the game I would spend a season following. Until, that is, during a West Texas visit to my ill father, it was suggested that I talk with eighty-six-year-old Robert Cramer, a retired geologist living in the tiny community of May.

He was working in his front yard on the late summer afternoon I met him, a man still agile and outgoing, eager to welcome the company of a stranger.

"I understand you grew up in Nebraska," I said as soon as handshake introductions were done.

"That's right. Lived in the little town of Hardy, population 320, until I went into the service."

"And you played six-man football in high school . . . "

"Yes sir. In fact, I played in the first six-man game ever played. So did my brother." For the next half hour, as we sat on his front porch enjoying an early evening breeze, he told me of a time and place not recorded on any electronic database.

He'd been a 156-pound high school senior in the fall of 1936, looking forward to another year of playing basketball and running the quarter mile on the track team, when he learned that Hardy High School was looking for volunteers to participate in a football game.

"It all started with the coach over at Chester, you know," he said. "He'd come up with the idea of playing football with only six men. He took the idea around to some other schools and got them to buy into his brainstorm."

It began, he remembers, as a combined effort of four schools in the rural south of Nebraska: Hardy, Chester, Alexandria, and Ruskin. "There was one team made up of kids from Chester and Hardy, another of students at Alexandria and Ruskin. We used hand-me-down equipment the coaches had gotten from some bigger schools and played the game on a field near a little college in Dechler. Best I can remember, there weren't even any goal posts—

which was just as well since none of us had any idea how to kick an extra point or field goal."

His coach, Milo Cameron, a tennis letterman from the University of Nebraska, had precious little knowledge of any kind of football, much less this newly invented game. "He just told us to run hard with the ball while we were on offense and tackle the other guy when we were on defense. I do remember that we did quite a bit of passing. And I turned an ankle pretty badly late in the game."

The final score? "I have no idea," he admits.

Clear memories of the farming community in which he spent his boyhood, however, sound as if it could have been a distant cousin to Penelope in its heyday. "Hardy had two grocery stores, two gas stations, a bank, a drugstore, a feed store, and a doctor's office," he says. "The business district was one block long." His father ran the local tavern–pool hall.

"There were eighteen students in my graduating class; twelve girls and six boys. Hardy doesn't even have a school today," says the lone living member of the Class of '36.

As the day faded toward dusk, my impromptu history lesson moved from the origin of six-man football to Cramer's World War II experiences, his migration to Texas during the oil boom days, and those times when he and his wife would be in the stands every fall Friday night to watch their son play six-man ball for the May High Bulldogs. "I haven't been to a game in several years," he said as he glanced up the street toward the high school. "Maybe this season I ought to get out to one."

With that he pulled a billfold from his hip pocket and began thumbing through small scraps of paper. "This is my brother's number," he says. "He played football in Hardy for a couple of years after I graduated. His memory might be better than mine."

The following day I phoned Bill Cramer, a retired teacher, at his home near Spokane, Washington. It had not taken long, he told me, for Hardy High School to develop into a six-man powerhouse, quickly eclipsing the efforts of Epler's Chester teams. "The year after that first game," he remembered, "they formed an eight-team league called the Little Blue River Conference. By my senior year (1938), six-man ball was being played all over Nebraska, and we won the state championship." A national magazine called *The American Boy* selected two Hardy players to its six-man all-America team.

One of them was Raymond Czirr, now eighty-three and a retired plant manager for Armor Foods. Living in Superior, Nebraska, just a half hour's drive from his hometown, Czirr remembers the games he and his teammates played as a diversion from the grinding agonies brought on by the Great Depression. "Times were pretty tough back then," he says, "but everybody in town got behind our team. We were the roaring pride of Hardy. By my senior year we even had a little football field behind one of the filling stations. People paid a dime to come watch our games.

"Football was important to the town. Hell, it kept the folks in Hardy going," he says.

A thousand miles away and three-quarters of a century later, many of those gathered to watch the Penelope Wolverines open their home season say much the same.

2

IT HAD BEGUN IN A BLUR OF ONE-HUNDRED-DEGREE AUGUST days, weeks before the opening of the new school year. Coach Corey McAdams had mailed out twenty letters, inviting potential young candidates to become part of the Penelope football program. On the day of the first preseason practice, only twelve stood in line to receive a uniform. Three others had promised to report once they'd finished helping their fathers harvest the summer grain crop.

Now, as McAdams and his assistants stood on the sidelines, watching while the enthusiastic players began calisthenics, Marvin Domesle's tractor rattled past in a neighboring field. The elderly farmer didn't wave. He and his brother, Joe, who own the property bordering the football field, had a long-standing reputation of being several handshakes shy of neighborly. The lifetime Penelope residents, in fact, had contacted superintendent Johnson on more than one occasion to grouse about kids climbing the fence guarding their field to reclaim errant footballs.

Neither the small turnout of players nor the thick cloud of dust floating in the wake of Domesle's tractor dampened McAdams's spirit as he prepared for the first practice. "To me," he had remarked to assistants Randall Ballew and Charles Bellows, "this is always the most exciting day of the season."

Trim and tanned from a summer spent hauling hay, McAdams spoke from experience. Son of legendary high school coach Royce McAdams, he'd quarterbacked his dad's Sudan High School team to the state championship in the mid-'90s, then gone off to play college ball at Abilene's Hardin-Simmons University. After graduating with a degree in communications, he'd taken a job as promotions director for a local television station but quickly wearied of the nine-to-five routine. And as he'd been doing throughout his life, he sought the counsel of his father. When his dad suggested a career in teaching and coaching, twenty-four-year-old Corey took him up on his advice.

His quest would lead him to a town he'd never heard of, to teach a brand of football he knew little about. Now preparing for his third season as head coach at Penelope, he'd not yet seen his team win.

And while the $8,000 he receives over his modest teaching salary is light-years shy of the six-figure salary reportedly earned a couple of hundred miles away by the football coach at perennial Class AAAA powerhouse Highland Park High, and though his job description requires that he teach a full course load of speech and health classes, coach both the high school and junior high teams, line the field for home games, and keep the team's uniforms laundered, McAdams seems to thrive on the workaholic demands of his position. Once football season ends he will assume responsibility for running the time clock at basketball games and drive an afternoon school-bus route. When spring arrives, he'll coach the boys and girls track teams—without benefit of a running track on which to practice.

The latter shortfall is no big deal in the make-do world of Penelope High athletics. The tennis team had won district the year before after being driven thirty-five miles daily to the Baylor University campus in Waco to find a court on which to practice. The golf team, meanwhile, had traveled to a Hillsboro municipal course to prepare for its schedule of tournaments.

In Penelope, the time-honored axiom about a-will-and-a-way can be loosely translated into if-the-kids-really-want-it-we'll-provide-it.

For now, however, it is football that has McAdams's undivided attention. A few weeks earlier he traveled to Lubbock to attend the annual Six-Man Football Coaching School, where for several days he went to seminars and lectures, listening and taking notes as his more experienced and successful peers from throughout the state spoke about offensive strategies, defensive alignments, favored practice drills, and motivational techniques. Once back home, he made revisions in the playbook he would hand out to his players, checked to see that all the equipment was in proper working order, and placed calls to make certain officiating crews had been assigned to the upcoming home games.

For two weeks before school's opening, I watched as his new team gathered each afternoon for practice. In truth, there is nothing glamorous or particularly fun about the routine of preparing for the season. Daily, the players do stretching and myriad agility routines, then a series of prepractice forty-yard dashes. That done, McAdams puts his players through offensive drills wherein plays are repeatedly run and blocking patterns taught. On the opposite end of the field, assistant Ballew teaches defense, which focuses on one-on-one tackling and pass defense. In Penelope, where the budget does not allow for mechanical aids like blocking sleds and tackling dummies, every aspect of the workouts pits player against player.

Ultimately there is a thirty-minute, gamelike scrimmage before the players again pair off to deal with such specialty functions as kickoffs, punts, and extra points. And then, just as the lungs and tired legs beg for it all to end, there are more dreaded forty-yard dashes.

And with each practice's end, there is the reminder that there will be another tomorrow. And tomorrow. I quickly recognized that if there was a difference in the methods of the Penelope coaches and those who drill teams on the practice fields of larger high schools throughout the state, it was an abundance of patience. Though there was the occasional bark that accompanies traditional coaching demands, I heard no demeaning comment when an inexperienced freshman or sophomore missed a tackle or dropped a pass. "We're out here to learn, to get a little better every day," McAdams constantly reminded. "If everyone works hard, we'll get it together; we'll be a team all of you can be proud of." Among those to whom he spoke were, frankly, only a few candidates with even the slightest degree of natural athletic ability.

But for better or worse, they would be the team. Three seniors, two juniors, five sophomores, and four freshmen.

Aware of the tragic news that a seventeen-year-old Dallas Carter High School senior had died of heat prostration just days earlier after a grueling three-hour practice conducted in one-hundred-degree heat, McAdams limited each practice to just over an hour and halted them at regular intervals for water breaks. An overweight sophomore, neither in shape nor familiar with the demands of conditioning, was watched closely.

Finally, after days of doing endless wind sprints and tackling drills and repeatedly running plays until all assignments were satisfactorily set in memory, the season would begin on a sultry Friday evening in an area of Texas that, in recent years, has become internationally famous. A fifteen-minute drive from the community of Oglesby, site of the season opener, was little Crawford, Texas, summer home of U.S. president George W. Bush.

If I left early for the game, I decided, I would have time to stop for a quick inventory of the disruption that had occurred in a small town that had once shared the same quiet obscurity enjoyed by Penelope and so many other little-known Texas hamlets.

The lone traffic light that slows passing motorists in the heart of Crawford blinked needlessly as I arrived near the end of the day. Most of the 705 residents of the now famed community had already made their way home or out to the high school to watch their own football team practice for its season opener.

Things had apparently returned to normal. A week earlier the president had left his nearby ranch and returned to the White House, taking with him the mob of reporters who had spent unhappy weeks camped out at the junior high gymnasium-turned-press-center, wondering whatever happened to the idea of presidents taking their vacations in the more cosmopolitan and comfortable climates of Kennebunkport and Martha's Vineyard.

For many of the year-round residents who bade the vacation and its accompanying hoopla farewell, there was a divided attitude of "good riddance" and "hurry back soon." President Bush and the attention he'd focused on Crawford since purchasing longtime resident Ken Engelbrecht's sixteen-hundred-acre ranch had been both a boon and burden. The economy of the former Tonkawa Indian campground-turned-cotton-ginning-center had been greatly boosted by travelers seeking keepsakes from the numerous souvenir shops that had sprung up in the downtown area or the chicken-fried-steak special at the Spano Family Coffee Station. To the civic-minded, Crawford was finally "on the map." On the other hand, Bush's Texas home had now become a magnet for the oddball crusaders of the world. Police chief Donnie Tidmore and his three-member staff have lost track of the number of protest marches, calling out against war, taxes, and environmental woes, that have paraded through their streets since Bush's election.

Mayor Robert Campbell, meanwhile, admits his weariness with giving interviews that never fail to result in lookalike stories that always point out that he is a black Democrat in a community that is 96 percent white and growing more Republican by the day. But like the police chief, Campbell says it is not the president, nor his Secret Service entourage, not even the often boorish members of the media that cause his greatest concern. "It's the protesters," he says, with little sympathy in his tone.

"What they are," an overall-clad listener standing nearby adds in less politically correct terms, "is a giant-sized pain in the ass." Others are simply local amusements, inherited "characters" who arrive with a multitude of political agendas.

Like sixty-seven-year-old Doc Mishler, the former Western Michigan University professor, who was sitting next to his horse, Chief Spirit, and dog, Czar Bear, resting beneath a shade tree near the post office. Dressed like a character out of *Lonesome Dove,* Mishler had ridden thirty-two hundred miles from his Montana home in an attempt to raise awareness of the starving children throughout the world. He would, he insisted, remain in Crawford, until he had the opportunity to speak personally to the president.

Meanwhile, he is quick to entertain with recollections of his adventurous journey, which had taken a full year, and the generosity of people he'd met along the way on what he calls his "final mission in life." "Given the opportunity," he told me, "I'm sure I can turn the president's attention from war to providing nutrition for future generations."

He's even got a gift for President Bush.

His trip, he explained, had begun with two horses he rode alternately. The mare, Faith, gave birth to a foal soon after he'd arrived in Crawford. He'd named the filly Hope. "If I ever get a chance to meet the president, I'm going to give her to him."

Knowing full well that his chance of ever speaking personally with the president was no better than mine, I wished him well and made a small donation to his cause.

It took but a short browse of downtown Crawford to realize it had become a Free World leader in per capita souvenir shops. In the event one is running low on George W. Bush T-shirts, coffee mugs, key chains, buttons, caps, postcards, pennants, or bobble-head dolls, the town's merchants stand ready to quickly meet the need.

During the month of August alone, lifetime resident Jamie Burgess, whose great-great-great-grandfather had been Crawford's first mayor, had welcomed customers from a dozen states and Canada into the Red Bull, a shop she and her mother operate. Daily, she explained, a steady stream of vacationers stop in to purchase proof they've visited the summer home of the president and listen to her complimentary history lesson. In short order, out-of-towners learn from her that Crawford once had a state-of-the-art hotel, a movie theater, a thriving livery stable, a damn fancy restaurant, and not one but two thriving cotton gins.

In a short time I'd heard and seen enough. Both fascinated and somewhat saddened by the political intrusion that had so abruptly rearranged the Crawford lifestyle, I was ready for a quick dinner before making my way on to Oglesby.

Yet even while I ordered the fried-catfish special and a glass of iced tea, there was no escaping the new history that hums through the town. Right over there, a young Coffee Station waitress said, is where President Bush and his wife, Laura, had sat just a few days earlier. At a table nearby, Secretary of State Colin Powell and National Security Advisor Condoleezza Rice had ordered their cheeseburgers. When Russian Federation leader Vladimir Putin had visited, he and members of his staff had stopped in for lunch.

On this evening, however, there were no celebrities. Only Jerry and Tami Melton and their blond-haired daughters, ages four and two, dressed in green-and-white Oglesby Tigers mascot uniforms, stood out in the crowd.

It took little eavesdropping to learn that Tami Melton was a teacher at Oglesby High and sponsor of the school's cheerleading squad. Keeping a tradition, she and her husband had driven to Crawford for an early dinner before attending the game. Intruding, I introduced myself and asked if they were looking forward to the beginning of the season.

"Absolutely," her husband replied as he lifted one of his daughters onto his lap. "We've been ready for it for months. This is the most exciting time of the year in Oglesby."

"Going to have a pretty good team this year?" I asked.

"Oh, yeah, I think so. Fact is, everybody's saying we ought to win really big tonight. The team we're playing hasn't won a game in years."

Penelope's reputation had preceded it, even to the summer home of the president of the United States.

Coach Ballew steered the yellow school bus along a winding Farm-to-Market road that led to the stadium, passing beneath a canopy of ancient pecan trees and, finally, scattering a wayward flock of chickens, which hurried from his path as he parked near the cinder block concession stand.

Soon the visiting Wolverines and Oglesby's Tigers were at opposite ends of the field, determinedly going through their pregame warm-ups. Near the stadium entrance, Melton, having arrived from Crawford, was distributing game programs, which her cheerleaders would sell before kickoff. And on a nearby table was a roll of twenty-five-cents-a-chance tickets for the raffle of a chocolate cake baked by a member of the local booster club. As the parking lot filled, there was good reason to believe that virtually all 450 residents of Oglesby would turn out for the season opener.

And on the opposite side of the field, a number of Penelope supporters—parents, teachers, students, a few ex-students—were gathering. Among the early arrivals was Clifton Darden, who had driven over from his home in Hubbard. He was anxious to see what progress the team had made since the days when he was its coach.

"We're getting better," the smiling McAdams said as he briefly broke away from pregame drills to greet his former mentor. It was Darden who had served as the Penelope coach when the football program was restarted. In Darden's second season, McAdams, having decided to work toward getting his teaching certificate, had volunteered to serve as his assistant.

The old coach smiled at his protégé and shook his hand. "You gotta remember," he laughed, "that I left you a lot of room for improvement."

Darden had never even seen a six-man football game when old friend Harley Johnson contacted him in that spring of 1999, asking if he would be interested in coaching at Penelope the following year. Darden, who hadn't coached in eleven years, quickly declined, explaining plans he'd already begun making for his retirement. Johnson, having reached the stage of his education career where he, too, was beginning to look forward to the time when he would no longer deal with the daily demands of overseeing the activities of the school, had pressed the matter no further.

Instead, he offered the position to an assistant coach at nearby Coolidge.

The young coach, eager for the early opportunity to advance his career, quickly accepted and spent the early part of the summer ordering the necessary equipment and making endless phone calls to arrange a last-minute schedule of games. Then, with the new school year almost at hand, he had telephoned Johnson to tell him that the head football coach at Coolidge had suddenly left and he'd been offered the job.

Suddenly without a coach, the Penelope superintendent resigned himself to the fact that football would have to be postponed for a year. Then, only a few days before he was to make the disappointing announcement, Darden had called. "I hear you lost your coach," he said. "I guess if you're going to have a team I'd better get on over there and help you."

With that, Darden went in search of a rulebook and made phone calls to old friends with experience at the new game he'd agreed to coach. "I didn't have a clue," he admits. "All I really knew was that six-man football was wide open and high-scoring, something I knew I was going to have a hard time getting used to." Throughout his lengthy career, he'd earned a reputation as a defensive-minded coach, winning a half dozen district championships primarily because he was able to successfully design ways to shut down the opposing teams' offense.

"I had no idea what an education I was about to get," he admits.

It hadn't occurred to him, for instance, that he would be required to deal with such rudimentary matters as instructing the inexperienced members of his team on the basic rules of the game, such fundamental exercises as how to properly block and tackle, even how to put on a uniform. Or to explain to overzealous parents that their place was in the bleachers and not on the sidelines, alternately encouraging and scolding their youngsters as a game was under way.

Having come to take so many things for granted during his coaching career, he suddenly felt as if he was speaking in a foreign language. When there is no tradition upon which to build, no past experience on which youngsters can draw, the demands coaches are wont to make fall on deaf ears.

On one Friday as he began preparations for the evening's game, Darden had been unable to locate Tanner Svacina, his starting quarterback. "I was worried that he might be sick or something, so I checked with his teachers and called his home but couldn't find him anywhere. Finally, one of our players nonchalantly mentioned to me that he'd left with his dad for a weekend hunting trip to Colorado or somewhere."

In Penelope, Darden quickly realized, priorities were different. It wasn't uncommon for a player to miss practice because he was needed in his father's fields or had been called on to help load cattle for a trip to market. Tolerance became a necessary tool. "In larger schools," he says, "there is a tough discipline, a commitment on the part of the kids and their parents, attached to the game. You practice or you don't play. You make the necessary sacrifices or you're off the team. You follow the rules to the letter or else. It's all part of the learning experience that comes from being involved in athletics. Everything's pretty black-and-white."

For the first time in his career, Darden found himself constantly in gray areas, adjusting his philosophy, forced to remind himself repeatedly that the youngsters he was coaching had no real concept of the demands of the game. To him it might have been all about winning and losing; to them it was just another way to pass the time and briefly escape the small-town boredom.

"One of the first rules you learn at the six-man level," he says, "is to keep enough kids on the team so you can play out the schedule. It really doesn't matter if they have much athletic ability. If they make passing grades and behave themselves, they're an important part of your team. When the talent pool is shallow, you make do with what you have."

When no other teachers volunteered to assist him, Darden had recruited the help of his daughter, Vicki, a junior high math teacher at Penelope. In the afternoons she served as an assistant coach; then on Friday nights she filmed the games that her dad would later study. His son, teaching in Waco, agreed to scout upcoming opponents, paying for his weekly trips out of his own pocket.

Darden and his thirteen Wolverine players launched the school's new football history with ten straight lop-sided defeats. And by season's end he realized that the experience had been the most enjoyable of his coaching career. When Johnson asked if he would consider staying on for one more season, Darden didn't hesitate. The bonus he would receive was a full-time assistant.

Corey McAdams, he was told, was working toward his teaching certificate and would be serving as a substitute in the spring and teaching full time in the fall. He'd already expressed interest in helping with the football program. Darden, aware of the impressive coaching reputation of Corey's father, looked forward to working with and grooming his son.

It was in that second season that the Wolverines, still raw and inexperienced, scored their first victory. The opponent was Cranfills Gap, and a freshman running back named Michael Lozano had led the scoring as Penelope won, 32–20. Then, in the immediate wake of his moment of glory, he had abruptly quit the team.

Having slightly injured a knee, the youngster became worried that he might not be at full speed when basketball season got under way.

━━━━━━━━

Still, that lone win had clearly signaled progress upon which McAdams, who would inherit Darden's job the following fall, could build.

Earlier in the week, while his team practiced, I roamed the cool halls of Penelope's old red-brick school building, pausing to view the contents of the dusty trophy case that told of past achievements. There was a photograph of a smiling group of teenagers who had won the 1954 state girl's basketball championship, trophies won in volleyball tournaments and at cross-country meets, and large plaques attesting to the fact that Penelope High School had performed the best one-act play in Texas on several occasions. There was also an impressive winning record of both district and regional titles.

In a far corner, almost hidden, was the only evidence of football good fortune. The game ball from that lone victory in 2001 bore the faint signatures of those who had played in the historic game.

There was nothing, however, that answered the following question: How had the school adopted the wolverine as its mascot when there was no record of the ferocious little badgerlike carnivore ever roaming Hill County? I had heard only one mildly satisfactory explanation, which had been handed down from the '40s. Back then, the story went, boys who relentlessly chased girls were often referred to as "wolves." Somehow the stretch from wolf to wolverine was made. As Barbara Minze, editor of the nearby Hubbard newspaper, tells it, the kids simply "thought it would be a neat name to use as a mascot." Just, I suppose, as folks up at the University of Michigan did when they christened their athletic teams with the same nickname—again, without evidence that the wolverine was indigenous to their state.

Whatever the case, wolverines seem a more thoughtful selection than that made in nearby Itasca, where proud townspeople somehow manage to maintain a straight face when they refer to their community as the "Home of the Fightin' Wampus Cats."

3

A LTHOUGH IT IS NOT UNUSUAL FOR THE SPORTS SECTIONS OF Texas newspapers to devote countless column inches to coverage of high school football, news of the six-man game is passed along primarily through the efforts of an Austin man who has established himself as something of an underground guru and self-appointed expert.

Granger Huntress, a forty-year-old communications manager for the U.S. Tennis Association, is the keeper of a Web site—sixmanfootball.com—on which he posts schedules and scores, provides weekly team rankings, and offers a busy chat room for fans. ("Hey, all you Bulldogs fans out there. Get ready for a kick-ass season. We're loaded this year . . . ") Huntress's knowledge of the game is encyclopedic. Want to know the score of the 1979 six-man Texas state championship game between Milford and Cotton Center?

He can give it to you off the top of his head. Historical milestones and oddities? He'll tell you that tiny Marathon, far out in the isolated Big Bend region, once enjoyed the glory of going fifty games without a single defeat but, alas, last year had to forfeit all of its games since only three players reported for the team. Remember '95, when little Mullin High played a Colorado school from Weldon Valley for the mythical six-man national championship? Huntress was there, notebook in hand, roaming the sidelines.

For years it has been his weekly routine to attend at least one game in person, ofttimes two. "I try to see fifteen or twenty games a season," he says, pointing out that his travel plans are Lone Star State simple: "I look for the good games that will be played near someplace where I can get good barbecue."

The color and atmosphere of the rural sport fascinate him. "All the wonderful clichés are there: community pride, school spirit, great people. I love it," he says.

He held out little hope, however, that good fortune would soon visit Penelope. In his preseason ratings of the 112 Texas teams that would open the 2004 season, the Wolverines were ranked No. 107. It was, then, no surprise to Coach McAdams when he paid a midweek visit to Huntress's Web site and learned that his team would enter its season opener as a decided underdog.

The opening game's early going mirrored Huntress's dire prediction. The Penelope offense, obviously tense, fumbled the ball away on the first series of downs. On the next play a face mask penalty was called against the defense. Three minutes into the game, Oglesby scored its first touchdown.

Even before the first quarter ended, Paul Lozano had left his seat in the bleachers to alternately pace nervously and lean against the fence that bordered the playing field. A single father who had moved his family to Penelope five years earlier, he knew full well the high hope and determination his son had brought to his senior year.

Michael, after giving up football midway through his freshman season, had returned as a sophomore and had been the Wolverines' offensive star ever since. As a junior he had been named to the all-district team and now, in his last year, hoped that he might perform well enough to perhaps attract the attention of some small college coach willing to consider the possibility that a five-ten 150-pound running back could make the transition from six-man to eleven-man ball.

Handsome, with deep and brooding brown eyes, he is clearly the most athletically gifted of the Wolverines. His walk exudes a confidence that borders on aloof self-importance, and the ease with which he carries out the practice assignments ordered by the coaches is a source of some resentment on the part of his less gifted teammates. On those rare occasions when the region's newspapers mention Penelope games, it is generally the scoring feats of Lozano that are printed, without mention of those who hand him the ball or provide clearing blocks for his long and often dazzling runs.

Mixed with the normal dose of teammate jealousy, however, is the knowledge that it is Lozano's superior talent that offers the Wolverines their best chance of success. Whatever private envy might exist is overshadowed by a respect for the determination the A and B student brings to his performance. For him, games are played to win.

Which is to say he's come a long way since those junior high days when he'd attended a much larger school in the Fort Worth suburb of Everman. There, where drugs and gang activity had become a growing problem, Michael had fallen in with the wrong crowd, his grades had suffered, and discipline had become an ongoing battle. Thus Paul Lozano had begun looking for a new job that would take him back to the quiet comfort and safety of the community in which he'd grown up.

There had been a time when he, too, had hoped to continue his athletic career beyond the high school level. An outstanding point guard on the Penelope basketball team, he had, upon graduation, tried out for several junior college coaches before a knee injury ended his dream. With that he had dismissed thoughts of higher education, got married, begun working long hours for short wages, had a family, and ultimately divorced.

The thirty-nine-year-old father wanted something better for his teenage son. On this day, as he's done throughout Michael's high school career, Paul made the 120-mile round trip to his job at a box-making factory in Temple.

As the second quarter got under way he cheered as Michael raced around right end, outran several would-be tacklers, and scored to bring the Wolverines into a 6–6 tie. It would, alas, be as close to victory as they would come.

Another fumble led to a second Oglesby touchdown. Then quarterback Kyle McCabe threw an interception that resulted in another. It was clear the game was slipping away from the smaller and outmanned Penelope squad. By the end of the third quarter, Oglesby fans were celebrating a 41–6 advantage.

Then, as the fourth quarter got under way, the elusive Lozano, despite playing with a badly jammed finger, scored three quick touchdowns. With just over two minutes remaining, the deficit had been cut to 47–24.

As Oglesby again drove down the field, Wolverines lineman Mason Ewell received a jarring hit in the back and lay on the field, attended by the coaches. Leaning against a nearby fence, his brother, Morgan, who had played for Penelope throughout his high school days, was urging his younger sibling to get on his feet. "Get up, man. We need you. You gotta go. Be tough."

Mason, however, limped to the sidelines and Oglesby scored again with just two minutes to go in the game. Only

two seconds remained when quarterback McCabe completed a short pass to Lozano, who ran in for his fifth touchdown of the evening. Final score: Oglesby 55, Penelope 30.

The loss took its toll on the small group of weary and
sweat-soaked players huddled around the Penelope
coaches at one end of the field. The knuckle on Lozano's
jammed finger was badly swollen. Mason Ewell and Kyle
McCabe nursed bruises to their rib cages. A badly sprained
ankle, which had also forced sophomore Josh Hampton to
limp to the sidelines late in the game, was the cause of the
grimace on his face as Coach McAdams spoke.

"I don't want to see anybody with his head down," the
coach said. "You played hard and I'm proud of that. We
made some mistakes, but we can fix that. We're going to get
better."

And then he reminded them that one of the pregame
goals had been accomplished, that at least a small victory
had been won: "You played four quarters against a good
team," McAdams pointed out. The dreaded "mercy rule"
defeat, the most embarrassing way to lose a game, had
been avoided.

As the stadium lights were being turned out, we parted
company, the team off to a Whataburger in nearby Waco
for a postgame meal, me to make a long full-moon drive out
to West Texas to check on my ailing father.

Football has been an important part of my family's life for as long as I can remember. In boyhood I had been fascinated by the firsthand stories of my dad's derring-do as a fleet halfback for his old Bastrop High Bears, never once wondering if perhaps his tales of long, winding touchdown runs and game-saving tackles might have become a bit overseasoned by the passage of time. (One of my proudest possessions, in fact, is the old block letter B he'd received back in the fall of 1936. It hangs proudly on my wall, encased in a shadowbox frame.)

When my own less stellar playing days finally came around, he was a dutiful traveler to each of my games, always quick to praise, win or lose. Our Thanksgiving dinners were always scheduled around the day's televised football games. Same with all autumn Sundays. When the sermons of a Southern Baptist preacher whose name escapes me became a bit too long-winded, it was Dad who decreed a spiritual sabbatical was in order so no kickoffs of Dallas Cowboys games would be missed. He cheered them on Sundays with the same vigor he focused on his beloved University of Texas Longhorns on Saturdays. And his midweeks were filled with reflections on games previously played and predictions on those upcoming.

I think, frankly, that the only real understanding my father ever had of the profession I'd chosen came during the years I was assigned to cover the Dallas Cowboys for the *Dallas Morning News*. There, I'm convinced he'd decided, was a noble calling worthy of the same coffee shop boasts he made of his other son, who, after his own playing days ended, had become a successful high school coach.

Dad listened with delight when I first told him of my new undertaking. To him, following and writing about the Penelope football team made far greater sense than the books about tangled crimes and social tragedies I'd been doing for too many years.

Then, just as the season was to get under way, he'd become critically ill, the victim of a multitude of old man frailties and malfunctions. His once bright eyes became dull, his always-tanned skin pallid, his steady voice quieted to a whisper. And I had to come to grips with that grim reality no son anticipates: My father was dying.

And so, priorities suddenly reordered, I found myself spending more and more time at his side. Which was why Brownwood, Texas, was again my destination following the Wolverines' season opener.

The first hoarse question Dad asked upon my late night arrival was "How did Penelope come out?" The Wolverines clearly had a new and interested fan.

"They lost," I said. Then, pulling my notebook from my pocket, I relayed to him the details of the game.

"Maybe next week," he weakly replied.

Those words, it occurred to me, have fueled the hopes of thousands upon thousands of high school players and coaches and fans for as long as the game has been played. *Maybe next week.*

In Penelope, I assured him, that was always the hope.

———————

It was in those same wee hours that April McAdams was considering taking her pillow and slipping from the bedroom where her husband had finally fallen into a fitful sleep.

In his dreams, Coach McAdams was replaying the game, tossing, turning, and kicking away bed covers as he called out instructions to players and yelled at referees whose calls he clearly judged unfair.

Unwinding was always difficult for her husband. Routinely upon their return home he would telephone his father to see how his Little River Academy team had fared, then detail for him how Penelope had performed. He would review the videotape of the game, pace, record the game statistics his wife had kept, and finally settle in front of the television to channel-surf for a History Channel documentary or a mindless science fiction movie to watch.

April understands her husband's devotion and accepts it with great patience—until Sunday mornings. When Corey, sitting next to her in their regular pew at the Columbus Avenue Baptist Church, begins diagramming plays on the back of the church bulletin during the sermon, she quietly reaches over and takes away his pencil.

4

S MALL TOWNS HOLD JEALOUSLY TO THEIR LEGENDS. IN HICO, Texas, another of the state's countless railroad-stop–cotton-gin communities that has dwindled to less than fifteen hundred residents, they proudly offer passersby a different version of the life and death of the notorious Old West outlaw Billy the Kid. Historians insist that William Bonnie, aka The Kid, a deadly killer with a lengthy list of saloon brawls and shoot-out victims by the time he'd reached his twenty-first birthday, was shot down in 1881 by famed lawman Pat Garrett during a jailbreak attempt in Fort Sumner, New Mexico.

Folks in Hico argue that the real story is that The Kid dropped dead of a heart attack on a morning in 1950 while on the way to their post office. At the time he'd reached the ripe old age of ninety.

By then, according to Hico historian Bob Hefner, Bonnie had changed his name to Ollie (Brushy Bill) Roberts and settled in the Central Texas community, where he shared the secret of his true identity only with the closest of friends. Whether you believe it or not, it's a damn fine yarn and now provides the only bona fide tourist attraction in town—the Billy the Kid Museum.

On the morning following their loss to Oglesby, coaches McAdams and Ballew had traveled to Hico, not for a lesson in Texas folklore but to attend what was being billed as "Six-Man Super Saturday."

The brainchild of local brothers Mike and Jim Ferguson, the day-long football festival, complete with a parade, a proclamation from the governor, and an appearance by the most celebrated six-man player in Texas history, was being held to raise funds for a new field house for the Hico high school. Three games were scheduled at the old native-rock stadium, and fans were arriving from all directions to watch teams from Aquilla, Zephyr, Rule, Strawn, Calvert, and Gordon open their seasons.

And it wasn't just the fans of those schools invited to compete who made the trip. A carload of urbane-looking Fort Worth lawyers, who for years had been making regular outings to six-man outposts, arrived early and were buying souvenir T-shirts even before finding a spot in the stands from which to view the day-long competition. Curiosity seekers from as far away as Abilene and Dallas filled the nearby Koffee Kup diner, ordering up the specialty of the house—saucer-sized homemade doughnuts—before traveling to the stadium to see what six-man football was all about.

For McAdams and Ballew, the purpose was to scout the archrival Aquilla High Cougars, a team they would face once the District 15 schedule got under way. Ballew thumbed through a program and began shaking his head as he called out the weights of some of the Aquilla players: "Listen to this," he said, "240 . . . 225 . . . 205 . . . 190 . . . 190. . . . Man, we've gotta start feeding our kids better." The only two-hundred-pounder on the Penelope roster was sophomore Josh Young, a substitute end who was not likely to see much playing time.

McAdams nodded in agreement as his eyes wandered to the far edge of the field, where a trim, balding man stood, talking with officials in charge of the event. "There's Jack Pardee," he announced, making no attempt to disguise his admiration.

———

For a sport that has produced but a handful of players who have gone on to play at the collegiate and professional level, Jack Pardee has long reigned as the poster boy of Texas six-man football. From the playing field of tiny Christoval High in the early '50s, he'd gone on to Texas A&M, where he'd starred for the legendary Paul (Bear) Bryant.

Then, for fifteen years he'd labored as a standout line-backer for the Los Angeles Rams and Washington Redskins. Later, he'd served as head coach for the Chicago Bears, the Redskins, and the Houston Oilers.

Now retired, Pardee was on hand to serve as the event's honorary referee.

And as he waited to toss the coin for the first game, he reminisced about a time a half century earlier when his father, suffering so badly with rheumatoid arthritis that he could no longer work, had moved his family to Texas from the Iowa farm he'd been forced to sell. Tiny Christoval's mineral baths and arid climate, however, had worked a miracle on the ailing Earl Pardee. The arthritis cured, he was soon able to resume farming and did so for another forty years. And he'd watched proudly as his son grew into the school's premier athlete.

In truth, there wasn't a great deal of competition for the honor. "There were only twenty-seven kids in the whole high school," Pardee says. "We had eight in my graduating class." The field where he and his teammates played their long-ago Friday night games had doubled as the local rodeo arena. "It was right on the banks of the South Concho River," he recalls, "and people would just drive their pickups right up to the field and sit in them, watching our games."

In the 1952 regional championship against Fort Davis, they saw Pardee run and pass for nine touchdowns as the Cougars completed an 11–0 season.

And even now, after a remarkable career played out in front of sellout collegiate and NFL crowds, as well as All-America, All-Pro, and Coach of the Year honors, those long-ago games against such hamlet rivals as Mertzon, Garden City, and Forsan remain touchstone moments.

Looking out onto the field where teams were going through pregame warm-ups, he pointed to a young player obviously too small and too slow to play the game at any higher level. "That kid right there is a perfect example of what six-man football's all about. Of what small-town life's all about. He's thrilled to death to be a part of that team. And I'll bet you he's doing the same kinds of things I did back when I was his age: roaming the country, fishing, hunting, swimming, hanging out with his buddies. And his parents aren't worried about him, just so long as he gets home by dark. Youngsters who don't have that opportunity, that kind of freedom, are being cheated out of some wonderful experiences."

It was then that one of the coaches broke from his team's preparation for a moment and came toward Pardee. "I just wanted to say hello and shake your hand," he said before hurrying back to his team.

"You know, I had the good fortune to play college ball for a man considered one of the greatest coaches of all time," Pardee says. "And I also played for some of the best when I was in the NFL. But in all honesty, G. W. Tellerson, my coach back there in Christoval, had the greatest influence on my life of anyone I've ever known. He taught me a lot more than how to play football."

———

Just a few days earlier I'd heard Penelope High School English teacher Mike Baker suggest much the same about Corey McAdams.

It had been Baker's serious illness four years earlier that had prompted his taking a two-month leave of absence. A longtime friend of McAdams's father, he'd learned that Corey was interested in teaching and had recommended him as his substitute. In time, Baker, in his mid-fifties, and the young teacher-coach had become close friends.

When McAdams became the Wolverines' head coach, he'd approached Baker with concern that there was no public address announcer for home games. "He felt it was important that the kids hear their names called out when they made a good run or caught a pass or made a tackle, and he asked if I'd be willing to do it."

Thus Baker had become the "Voice of the Wolverines," doing pregame introductions of the local players and their opponents, calling out the names of those who made outstanding plays, and reminding fans of the lengthy menu being offered at the nearby concession stand. On those Friday nights when no volunteer stepped forward, Baker offered up an a cappella rendition of the National Anthem.

More important, he became an occasional sounding board and adviser for the young football coach trying to build a program.

"There was a time when I worried that whatever career plan he'd outlined for himself might suffer if he stayed in Penelope too long. Most coaches I've known begin at small schools, hoping to build a reputation that will lead to better jobs and better pay in bigger programs. My concern for Corey was that if he kept going without any wins year after year, he'd reach a point where there would be no opportunities left for him."

It is impossible, Baker suggests, to include on a résumé the difficulties McAdams had dealt with in the first couple of years he'd served as head coach. How do you explain that it wasn't an injury or even grade failure that kept one of your starters out of the lineup during a crucial game, but the family's insistence that the badly needed player skip the game and accompany them to the out-of-town wedding of a relative? In a community without knowledge of the game and its unwritten protocol, what do you say to a parent who casually strolls into the sideline huddle to offer a coaching suggestion while a game is under way?

"He wants to win as badly as anyone I've ever met," Baker says, "but as I've watched him my concerns over how his won-loss record might affect him have faded. He likes what he's doing. He loves these kids. And they respect him.

Like any school, big or small, we've got students badly in
need of role models, father figures. Corey's become that to
a lot of them. They're learning a lot more from him than
how to play football."

For Corey McAdams, Baker believes, coaching the
Penelope Wolverines is a calling.

———

Watching as Aquilla triumphantly opened its season with
an impressive display of speed, depth, and talent was a
sobering experience for McAdams and Ballew. There was
little valid comparison between the team they'd just
watched play and the one they were coaching. Following
the game they sought out the Cougars' coach, Benny
Weaver, to offer their congratulations.

"Hey, I hear you guys really got after Oglesby last night,"
Weaver generously responded. "Keep up the good work.
And best of luck."

As McAdams and Ballew walked toward the parking lot,
it was Ballew who broke a long silence. "When we play
those guys," he said, "we're going to need every damn bit of
luck we can get."

5

ONE OF PENELOPE'S MOST POPULAR TEACHERS, MIKE BAKER daily revisits his own childhood en route to his classroom. There, he can point out as he takes an early-morning walk down the echoing hallway, is where he was sitting, a seventh-grader taking a math test, on that November day in 1963 when the principal stuck his head through a raised window to inform his teacher President John F. Kennedy had just been shot and killed while riding in a motorcade in Dallas.

"Mrs. Walker burst into tears," he recalls, "then quickly composed herself and instructed us to continue with the test she was giving."

The son of a sharecropping farmer, Baker remembers when he and his brothers were the only non-Czech students in the entire Penelope school system, when the community still had an operating grocery store and gas station, when the largest class he'd been a part of numbered just sixteen students.

His story is similar to that of many of the community's elders, one of growing up in the bucolic Hill County environment, finally leaving in pursuit of higher education and a big-city job, then eventually returning to a place sorely missed.

Today, he teaches children and grandchildren of former classmates. But not before a lengthy visit to the outside world, where he'd sampled the urban lifestyle and ultimately judged it lacking.

Following graduation from Baylor University, he'd spent thirteen years in Dallas, working in the regional employment office for Sears. Along the way there was a marriage that went sour, the realization that he didn't know any of his neighbors, a disdain for traffic jams and crowded shopping malls, and, finally, a growing desire to escape it all. When his father died suddenly and his mother needed help back home, Baker had the reason he needed to return to his heartland.

Buying a home in nearby Hubbard, next door to the grand-niece of local legend and major league baseball great Tris Speaker, he began a six-year teaching career there. When, however, he learned that Penelope High was in need of a junior-high–high-school English instructor, he applied for and was offered the job. And for the past five years he's daily made the twenty-minute drive down Farm Road 2114 to his workplace, back to the simplicity and comfort of his boyhood days.

"I'm not a unique example," he is quick to point out. "There are people in Penelope who still live within five miles of where they were born. Others went away for a time and have now returned." There are, he notes, high school seniors he teaches who began their educational journey together in the first grade.

For all its economic drawbacks, social isolation, and daily struggles simply to remain in existence, there is something magnetically special here. Baker, perhaps more aptly than anyone I became acquainted with, explains. To appreciate the rural lifestyle, he says, pleasures must come in the comfort derived from a simple and uncomplicated way of life. In Penelope, he says, there is no class system among the adults, no cliques among the small population of students. "I'd be hard-pressed to tell you the name of the wealthiest person in town. That's just not important. No one's trying to impress anyone here. Everyone buys their clothes at Wal-Mart; at every gathering, barbecue is the main item on the menu; and the social life of the entire community revolves around the school. And maybe most important of all, people are quick to help others in time of need.

He recalls the lengthy recovery from the surgery that kept him out of the classroom for most of a semester: "One afternoon, I woke from a nap and went into the kitchen. There on the table was an envelope with two hundred dollars in it. A note that accompanied it read, 'For the flowers we didn't send and the food we didn't bring by.' It was from a family whose home I'd only been in once in my life."

The benefactor's quiet entry into his home had been easy. Baker, like most, feels no need to lock his doors.

When a Penelope husband and wife simultaneously fell victim to cancer, the local Catholic church held a fundraiser during which ten thousand dollars was raised in a single day. When, last spring, the mother of a student was killed in an automobile accident, her son was immediately taken into the home of another family so he might remain in Penelope to complete the school year.

Such examples of adult charity have not gone overlooked by the young people of the community. "The last thing I want to do is paint a Camelot-like picture," Baker warns, "but the kids here genuinely care about each other. I see it every day in the classroom and in the halls. A pat on the back, a high-five, a hug. Whether you're on the football team or the volleyball team, whether you're getting ready to show an animal at the county fair or enter the poetry-reading competition at the district University Interscholastic League (UIL) meet, you're going to have the support of everybody in school. One person's success is everyone's success. It's part of a family-like atmosphere that is as remarkable as it is difficult to explain."

One which also extends to members of the faculty.

It is a daily routine for the coaches to gather in Baker's classroom during the lunch break, where, for a fast-passing half hour, they set aside the rigors of teaching and swap stories. On any given day, Ballew might be recounting a weekend hunting trip, Bellows bragging about some new accomplishment of his infant child, or McAdams bemoaning the latest Baylor Bears defeat he and his wife traveled to Waco to witness the previous Saturday. Baker generally clicks onto the Internet at the computer on his desk to see what late-breaking news event might merit discussion.

And naturally, there is talk of the next Saturday's Wolverines game. With the Oglesby defeat now history, thoughts turned to their next opponent, a small school on the outskirts of Dallas. Metropolitan Christian School, one of seventy-six private Texas schools that now field six-man teams, is an hour and a half's drive and light years removed from Penelope.

It is altogether safe to assume that no Metro student has ever driven a tractor, loaded a single bale of cotton, or shown a prize calf at the state fair. The Penelope Wolverines versus the Metro Christian School Eagles promised something more than just another football game. It would offer a distinct clash of cultures.

From its isolated rural campus, the Penelope team bus would have to wind its way into a foreign world—along congested highways, spurs and loops, past endless rows of high-rise businesses, sprawling apartment complexes, and a smorgasbord of fast-food restaurants to find the stadium in which it was to play.

"Sounds like it's going to be the country mouse against the city mouse," Baker joked as the lunch break was ending. Randall Ballew laughed. "More like Wal-Mart against Neiman Marcus," he suggested.

In recent years, private schools have proliferated in major cities as frustrated parents have given up hope that their children will receive a quality public school education. Add drugs, gangs, racial disharmony, lax discipline, and an army of burned-out, overworked teachers, and the stampede to safer, more academic-oriented climes was off and running for those moms and dads who could pay the price and for their children, if they were bright enough to gain admittance. The hand-picked students at Metro Christian, for instance, are allowed to enroll only after their admission applications are carefully screened and preenrollment testing is successfully completed. The annual tuition for high school students is $4,380, considered a bargain for safe passage into a scholastic climate in which the majority of teachers boast master's degrees.

Corey McAdams would be surprised to learn that he is greatly envied by Metro Christian coach Don McEvoy. A year earlier, McEvoy had taken his team to Penelope for a preseason scrimmage and came away impressed by the atmosphere he'd encountered. He liked the school, the community, and the relationship he'd seen between the coaches and players. The manner in which the inexperienced members of McAdams's team were working to overcome a history of defeat was inspiring. "Someday," McEvoy says, "I'd like to try a situation like the one in Penelope. I can't imagine a more rewarding coaching job."

This from a man whose team would enter the Saturday evening game ranked seventh among the state's private-school six-man teams and boasting a talented quarterback who was almost certain to celebrate a remarkable milestone at the expense of the Penelope defense.

For Corey McAdams, meanwhile, the game was important for a personal reason he'd not shared with his players or even his assistants. His father's team would be playing on Friday night, so Royce McAdams had made plans to travel to Dallas the following day to attend the Wolverines game. The elder teacher, an outgoing coach with a lengthy list of championship successes, was coming to check on the progress of his pupil, the quiet young man with whom he spoke by phone weekly, offering advice and encouragement.

Winner of 170 games during his twenty-seven-year coaching career, the elder McAdams knows better than anyone the competitive drive of his son. He loves telling the story of the time when the family lived in the Panhandle community of Whiteface, where his coaching career began. The McAdamses lived just across the street from the school, he remembers, and during the summer a set of monkey bars had been built on the elementary school playground. Corey, soon to enroll as a first-grader, announced to his father than his goal was to make it from one end of the bars to the other without stopping or losing his grip. "After the first day he had blisters all over his hands and I warned him not to overdo it. What he did the next day was wrap his hands in tape and go back at it. And he made it all the way across the bars." When there was a first-grade jump rope competition, Corey's nearest competitor dropped out after his count rose to fifty or so. Corey continued on well past two hundred before his dad convinced him to stop.

"He was one of those kids who always pushed himself. I can't say I taught him that. Nor did his mother. It's something he was born with."

The young McAdams broke his arm twice as an eighth-grader but missed few practices, so he was prepared for the day he would lead his father's Sudan High School team to the state finals as a sophomore, the state championship as a junior, and the semifinals as a senior.

Now in his mid-fifties and contemplating retirement from coaching, the burly Royce McAdams admits that his son was far from the most talented athlete he ever coached. "But," he adds, "I've never had one more dedicated."

April McAdams paced the sidelines of the picturesque little south Dallas stadium, clipboard in hand, watching as her husband and his aides put the team through its pregame warm-ups. Hardly the "football widow," April has, since her husband's venture into coaching, served as the official statistician, carefully logging the yardage of each run from scrimmage, the length of a completed pass, and tackles and interceptions made by each player. Unlike the other Penelope supporters making their way into the tree-shaded stands, April, as she traditionally does, had traveled on the team bus.

I doubt there is a bigger football fan. She is a Baylor graduate, and she and Corey rarely miss a home game of her downtrodden though beloved Bears. And on Sundays, they watch the Dallas Cowboys games together on TV. In preparation for the trip to Dallas she had tucked a tiny transistor radio into her jacket pocket so she could tune in to the broadcast of her college alma mater's game.

On this evening, however, there would be little time for anything but keeping track of the Ping-Pong-like scoring that would take place. From the kickoff it was obvious that Penelope had put its season-opening jitters aside and was ready to play much better than it had a week earlier. On the third play of the game, Lozano burst through the Metro defenders, broke several tackles, and sprinted fifty yards for a touchdown.

By the end of the first quarter, Metro Christian had tied the score, but not before a determined effort on the part of the Wolverines defense.

Early in the second period, Penelope fan Thomas Overby was on his feet, fists in the air, cheering stepson Joe Rendon's catch of a Lozano-thrown touchdown pass that put the visitors back into the lead. "We're gonna win this one," he said. "I believe we're gonna win it." The improved play of the Wolverines was but one reason for Overby's celebration. His stepson, a senior, was playing football for the first time and seeming to enjoy it. In previous years he had indicated interest in playing, even joining the team for a few preseason practices in his freshman and sophomore years, but had quickly lost interest and turned in his uniform. Now, however, he'd finally made the commitment and was fast becoming an important part of the team.

For the remainder of the half, the lead seesawed back and forth as Metro running back Marty Spakes scored on a couple of long runs. But shortly before the half, Penelope pulled within two points as sophomore Kevin Altamirano scored his first touchdown of the season. At halftime the Wolverines trailed by only 28–20.

It was early in the third quarter when the Metro quarterback, a lanky, strong-armed senior who was being recruited by several small colleges, established the record that the Eagles fans had come hoping to see. As he lofted a long, perfect spiral that resulted in a touchdown, the public address announcer waited briefly for the cheering to subside before making his breathless announcement. "Ladies and gentlemen," he said, "Eagles quarterback Wally Beaty has just thrown the one-hundredth touchdown pass of his high school career."

The two-touchdown margin was too much for the Wolverines to overcome. A Kyle McCabe–to-Lozano touchdown pass narrowed the gap early in the fourth quarter, but by game's end Metro Christian had scored a 52–32 victory.

Even in defeat, it was the best McAdams had ever seen his team perform. As the players huddled around him at midfield, the emotionally drained coach held his thumb and forefinger an inch apart. "You guys were this close," he said. *"This close.* I'm so proud of what I saw out there tonight. The effort . . . the improvement . . . the teamwork . . . the fact you took the fight to them."

Coach Ballew then led the team in a brief prayer. Head bowed, he did not see the tears that welled in the eyes of the spent McAdams.

Metro coach McEvoy stood to one side, waiting until the prayer was completed, then extended his hand to the Penelope coaches. "You guys mind if I say something to your kids?" he asked.

Stepping into the circle of kneeling players, he nodded his head silently for several seconds. "You boys gave us all we could handle," he said. "You're one tough bunch. Believe me when I tell you you're getting there. It's going to happen for you . . . real soon."

Near the team bus, Royce McAdams stood, waiting for his son, smiling broadly as he approached. He, too, was nodding approval. "Great game," he said as he draped an arm over Corey's shoulder. Then they embraced and the father whispered the words every son lives to hear. "I'm proud of you," the elder McAdams said.

———

While the second Penelope defeat of the season was being suffered quietly, another, thousands of miles away, was being reported by the wire services and broadcast on the late news. In Seattle, Washington, Bellevue High School had scored a 39–20 upset victory over Concord, California's De La Salle High as a crowd of twenty-five thousand looked on.

The De La Salle Spartans had won 151 consecutive games, the longest high-school winning streak on record. Not since 1991, when the senior members of the team were in kindergarten, had the Spartans been beaten.

Reading about it in the next day's paper, Randall Ballew wondered aloud how it was remotely possible for any team at any level to remain undefeated for such a remarkably long time. McAdams posed a different, more philosophical, question. How difficult, he wondered, was it to deal with defeat after a lifetime of nothing but victories?

6

IT WAS JUST PAST 7:30 ON FRIDAY MORNING, AND CALVIN Pratka had dropped his three elementary-aged grandchildren off in front of the Penelope school, watching as fourth-grader Zachary, third-grader Victoria, and kindergartner Colton joined the squealing parade of other children hurrying toward another day of learning. A driver for Waco-based Central Truck Lines for twenty-seven years, Pratka had a few minutes to spare before beginning his drive down Interstate 35. Parking his pickup, he slowly walked to the southern end of the campus, shading his eyes from the bright morning sun. He wanted to have a look at Wolverine Field, the stadium where the team would open its home season.

"This," he finally observed as his eyes roamed the neatly mowed turf, the shiny metallic bleachers, the press box painted in school color red, the lights, and the small electronic scoreboard, "is really something."

For all its recent won-lost futility, Penelope High football has come a long way since those days in the late '50s and early '60s when the son of the onetime local feed store owner had played the game.

From 1958 until Pratka's senior year in 1963, football had been a part of the school's extracurricular activities. But not until the midway point of his final season had Penelope finally won a game, defeating Venus, 32–12. The same Venus High that a few years earlier had, in the days before Texas had adopted the forty-five-point mercy rule, humiliated Penelope, 110–0.

"We never had more than eight or nine kids on the team," he remembers, "and didn't even have a place to play." Pointing in the direction of the nearby stock tank that now provides irrigation for the Wolverines' field, he recalls practicing there in what was then only a rocky pasture. "We played all of our 'home' games over in Abbott's stadium back then."

It is neither moments of high drama nor Friday night glories that Pratka recalls from those days when he played and his graduating class numbered only eight. "About all I can remember from back then," he says, "was a game against Tolar when I got a front tooth busted out and one against Trinidad when I was knocked unconscious on the opening kickoff and didn't remember a thing until halftime."

The boys in his graduating class were the last to play football as the school board voted to call it quits after a five-year record had plummeted to only one win and forty-six defeats. That's where Penelope's football history had been frozen until its revival thirty-six years later in the spring of 1999.

Pratka is glad to see the school again fielding a team. And for him and many of the townspeople, the new stadium is a symbol the struggling community had badly needed: a sign of commitment to the town's future. "This is a good thing," he observes as he turns to leave. "I don't think folks here at the school would have gone to the expense of building it if they didn't think Penelope was going to be around for a long time to come."

Just days earlier I'd been reading a *Dallas Morning News* article that detailed the staggering amount of money spent and earned by high school football throughout the state. The report estimated that on any given Friday night, the 1.2 million fans who weekly attend games would shell out an estimated $275 million for tickets, parking, programs, concession stand purchases, travel, meals, lodging, and booster club souvenirs.

Most impressive in the economic report, however, were the expenditures that large and even medium-sized school districts were doling out for the monolithic venues in which their teams played. In Denton, a newly completed football stadium with a seating capacity of twelve thousand had just been built at a cost of over $20 million. At the same time, the remodeling of Mesquite's stadium had set taxpayers back $9.8 million. In Southlake Carroll, a wealthy suburb north of Dallas, a $15-million stadium was only part of the expense heaped on the school's highly successful program. On days when winter weather threatens to hinder preparation for an upcoming game, the team works out in a million-dollar indoor practice facility, complete with the same artificial turf found in its outdoor stadium.

In Penelope, where break-even is the weekly goal, there is no evidence of such lavish excess.

Three years ago, when the school simultaneously applied for a state infrastructure facility grant and a modest bank loan with which to erect a new building that would house additional classrooms, a new gymnasium, and boys' and girls' locker facilities, the money needed for Wolverine Field was also included in the request. Total cost for the new state-of-the-art building that now adjoins the original school, two adjacent acres of land on which the football field was built, and the installation of bleachers, lights, and a scoreboard: $1.6 million.

Thanks to volunteer help in surveying, leveling, and cleaning the field; hauling in truckloads of sand; planting grass; and putting up fences—the building of Penelope's football stadium had required less than $20,000 of the grant and loan money awarded to the school district.

It might have been even less had not landowner Charlie Fabian, the lifelong Penelope resident whose granddaughter Audra is one of the Wolverines cheerleaders, lived up to his well-earned reputation as a hard-nosed businessman. A Norman Rockwell–like prototype of the rural Texas cowboy-rancher, he'd entered Harley Johnson's office one morning to finalize the sale of the small plot he'd agreed to turn over to the school. Leaning against his ever-present cane, he'd sent Johnson's hopes soaring when he'd said, "Aw, hell, since you people are going to use my land for a football field maybe I ought to just give it to you." Then, however, he'd grinned and tapped his cane against Johnson's desk. "'Course I'm not going to."

He did, however, eventually volunteer free use of water from his nearby tank for the newly sodded field, which he'd occasionally stop by to watch taking shape. One afternoon, as tractors moved and leveled dirt, he'd stood with Johnson and pointed his cane toward where the south end zone would eventually be. "You know," Fabian nonchalantly said, "there's a grave over yonder somewhere."

Johnson's face had immediately gone ashen as he contemplated all manner of legal and moral issues that would be in store. Soon, however, Fagan was laughing. "Yep," he told the relieved superintendent, "I buried ol' Cobra, my German shepherd, out there three or four years ago."

Although Cobra's bones were never discovered, dozens of shiny flint Indian arrowheads, relics from a far gone time in the region's history, surfaced as dirt was turned and smoothed.

Today, Johnson no longer even bothers to put a pencil to the annual cost of his school's football program. Over the course of a season, he's come to realize, tickets sold at Penelope home games will cover the cost of the use of the stadium lights, pay the stipend and mileage for referees, and buy the gas that fuels the team's out-of-town bus trips. By the time the concession stand profits and the revenue from the fifty-cent game programs are tallied, there might even be a small weekly profit.

"If we come out thirty or forty dollars ahead," he says, "that's great. At a lot of schools, that kind of money means nothing. Here, it does."

———

It is "Red Day," and classrooms are ablaze with school color. Cheerleaders arrive in uniform, looking forward to the morning pep rally, and members of the team wear their jerseys to class. Along the hallways, handmade banners of encouragement cover the walls.

During the forty-five-minute drive from their home in China Springs, April McAdams listened as her husband, usually quiet in the mornings, talked of the game plan that had been set in place for the opposing Gustine High Tigers. As in the previous two weeks, he spoke optimistically of the possibility of victory. The team that would travel 115 miles to Penelope, he acknowledged, was better, but not *that* much better. "All we need," he insisted, "is a break or two. They're coming here expecting to win. Expecting to forty-five-point us." Encouraged by the showing his team had made the previous weekend in Dallas, McAdams was confident that would not happen.

April was ready to do her part. At the beginning of the previous season she had organized the school's forty elementary students into what she now called her "Bleacher Creatures." To spread interest in football among Penelope's younger population and allow them an opportunity to be participants, she had suggested that her Creatures be introduced by public address announcer Baker before the kickoff of each home game as they formed a "spirit line" through which the Wolverines would run as they left the dressing room.

Now, she proudly points out, young students spend their recess periods choosing sides for quick games of pass-touch football, talking of the day they, too, will become members of the Wolverines team. They, she suggests, are the hope for the school's football future.

And since Penelope High School has never had a band, it hadn't bothered to adopt a school fight song, a tradition of virtually every high school in the country. April had therefore taken it upon herself to ask the China Springs school officials if Penelope might "borrow" theirs.

Thus, minutes before the kickoff, those seated in the packed bleachers and in lawn chairs along the fence, stood to follow announcer Baker's lead and sing: "The friends we've made while going here will last our whole life through/So to Penelope High and the Wolverines we pledge our hearts anew."

On this warm September night, with attendance at the game well in excess of Penelope's population, small-town football suddenly didn't seem all that different from the games that were being played elsewhere in huge stadiums filled with thousands of fans.

Students crowded around the concession stand, girls flirting with boys, boys flirting with girls, while waiting for soft drinks and hot dogs. On the grassy slope leading toward the field, parents spread blankets and urged their preschool children to quit their playing and get ready to watch the game. Some fans arrived with lawn chairs. Science teacher Berton Stengel was busy selling game programs while fellow teacher Kim Quiram gathered student members of her yearbook staff, suggesting photographs she wanted them to take during the game. Out in the parking lot, Harley Johnson was at his traditional post, directing late-arriving traffic toward the few remaining parking places.

There was about the place a bustling energy that belied the fact most had arrived with little hope of seeing the home team win. For all the legend and folklore surrounding Texas high school football and the not-so-frivolous suggestion that it ranks as a six-point favorite over Sunday-go-to-meeting in many small towns, its magical lure goes far beyond just cheering for winners.

In Penelope and the hundreds of communities like it, Friday night football is rural America's answer to a big-city block party.

———

Among those seated in the stands were Frank and Elizabeth Lewis, owners of the nearby Sunset Farm, where, since their move from Mississippi in 2001, they had raised and sold Tennessee walking horses.

It was during a trip to visit friends several years earlier that the route to their destination had carried them into Hill County. Elizabeth remembers it well: "Frank likes to get off the interstate and drive the back roads, and I was just looking out the window at the countryside. We came to this little rise, and suddenly you could see for miles and miles. The gently rolling landscape, the green fields and trees." The vista, she recalls, was breathtaking. "This," she'd told her husband, "is heaven."

Soon thereafter they began talking of moving west to rural Texas. Elizabeth's teenage daughter, Laura, was all for the move. Less enthusiastic about the plan was her son, Ben. Interested in neither the business of horse farming nor small-town life, he begged to stay in Mississippi with his father, Allen Patrick, a game warden living in the Jackson suburb of Crystal Springs. Finally, Elizabeth had reluctantly agreed.

The decision proved disastrous. Attending a large public school where he was able to quietly disappear into overcrowded classrooms, the unmotivated Ben Patrick performed poorly. At home, his father and grandmother fought an endless and unsuccessful battle to discipline the rebellious youngster. Ultimately pushed beyond frustration, Ben's dad sent him to live with his mother and stepfather. Life on a horse farm and in a rural school environment might offer a chance for what both parents agreed was a badly needed fresh start.

Since his arrival in Penelope in the summer weeks before the beginning of the new school year, Ben had struggled with only limited success to adjust to his new environment. He sulked, pined for the girlfriend he'd left behind, and made no secret of his dread of enrolling at an unfamiliar school.

His mother, then, had been pleasantly surprised one evening when Ben announced that a couple of boys he'd recently met—Kyle McCabe and Mason Ewell—were encouraging him to try out for the football team.

Now, preparing for her first look at six-man football, Elizabeth watched her son join his teammates in a final huddle before the game got under way, feeling a rush of pride as announcer Mike Baker introduced the Penelope players: "Number 4 . . . sophomore . . . Ben Patrick." She forced a smiled as she looked over at her husband. "Some of those players on the other team look awfully big," she observed. It was the mother's voice of worry for a son who, despite nearing six feet tall, weighed only 155 pounds. "He'll be fine," Frank Lewis assured her.

Elizabeth breathed deeply and nodded. Whether the Wolverines would win or lose was of little concern to her. That her son seemed to finally be fitting into his new environment was victory enough.

In their weekly telephone conversations, Royce McAdams had tried repeatedly to explain to his son that the greatest challenge a team with no tradition of winning faces is difficult to describe. And there is no coaching manual with a time-tested formula for dealing with the obstacle. "Somehow," he would say, "you've got to get your kids to a point where they not only believe they can win but know how to do it. It's that second part that's the hardest. If they've never had any experience with winning, what do you draw on for an example? The thing that scares hell out of every coach is the fact that it's so easy to get used to losing.

"You might be playing a team that's really not all that good, one that you have every chance in the world to beat. But unless your kids know how to get it done, believe they can do it, it's hard."

Corey McAdams, the father knew, was facing the most difficult obstacle their shared profession offers. How, the young coach had asked, do you teach confidence? "The way you're doing it," his father replied. "You just keep preaching to 'em."

In the first half, it quickly became clear that McAdams and his fellow coaches still had a great deal of preaching to do. Despite the team's improved performance against Dallas Metro, despite what they'd deemed a good week's practice, the Wolverines were terrible as the visitors scored on the opening kickoff and methodically built a 36–0 halftime lead. Fumbles, penalties, dropped passes, and missed tackles by the Penelope players had caused many in the stands to quietly turn their attention to conversation with their neighbors. The yell routines of the cheerleaders had become increasingly unenthusiastic. The embarrassment of a mercy-rule defeat was only a couple of scores away as the two teams made their way to the locker room.

Concerned that the game would not last much longer, Mike Baker quickly began running through the list of announcements that he'd been asked to make. "Don't forget," he told those in attendance, "that the Future Farmers of America's floral design class will be taking orders for mums for next week's Homecoming game."

At the end of the field, the Penelope coaches waited as their players, heads collectively bowed, marched to the dressing room. Several minutes passed before McAdams entered to try another tack. Usually soft-spoken, quick to emphasize the positives, he removed his cap, hurled it to the concrete floor, and let his anger show.

"You are *not* going to quit," he yelled at the youngsters slumped in front of their lockers. "Not this time, not like you've done in the past. Gentlemen, those days are over. If you don't want to go back out there and give it every ounce of effort you have, just stay in here." And with that he turned and walked out.

Moments later, a red-faced Kyle McCabe led the team as it literally burst from the dressing room. Inside, he'd stood to issue a challenge. "We're *not* going to embarrass Coach McAdams," he'd said. His teammates, high-fiving and butting helmets, began shouting the same resolve.

Soon, Lozano scored on a short run on Penelope's first possession of the half. Then Josh Hampton took a McCabe handoff on a reverse that surprised the Gustine defenders and raced into the end zone untouched. McCabe then lofted a long spiraling pass to Joe Rendon for another touchdown.

The renewed effort had not been enough to prevent a third straight defeat—Gustine would eventually triumph,

70–32—but face had been saved. "What you guys did in the second half . . . 32 points," Coach Ballew bragged afterward, "showed me something." It was, he praised, the best two quarters of football the team had yet played.

A now-calmer McAdams stepped forward to agree. "But we're going to put this one behind us the minute we walk off the field," he said. "We're going to forget it and start thinking about next week."

―――――――

There was another important piece of advice that McAdams's father had given him: "Son," he had said, "be careful when you make out your nondistrict schedule every year. If at all possible, find yourself a 'patsy' or two to play along the way. If you don't, you wind up being everybody else's 'patsy.'"

Indeed, for the past several years, virtually every team Penelope visited had eagerly scheduled its Homecoming activities to coincide with the arrival of the winless Wolverines.

If, indeed, there had been a sure win built into Penelope's schedule, it loomed just a week away. For its own Homecoming, it would play a team in its first year of football. Waxahachie's Faith Family Academy, a small charter school, was, in the words of school board member and volunteer scout Willie Harlin, "pretty bad."

The slow-talking Willie Harlin has been scouting Wolverine opponents since McAdams became the head coach. Weekly, he travels to the site of future opponents' games, notebook in hand, to chart offensive and defensive sets, take note of tendencies, and diagram plays that the Penelope team can expect to see. On Saturdays the son of a former coach and long-time teacher Paula Harlin meets the coaches at the school when they arrive to review the video of the previous night's game and passes along his report.

It is, he admits, a nice diversion from his daily work as a Hill County juvenile probation officer, dealing with first-time offenders tiptoeing on the edge of serious trouble: kids busted for possession of marijuana, caught shoplifting in Hillsboro stores, or getting into fights at school; kids he describes as being totally apathetic about education and its value.

He can't, however, remember a time when a Penelope student has appeared in his office. "In fact," he says, "we rarely see kids from any of the towns in the southern part of the county."

In the rural outposts, he explains, there is a built-in warning system that generally short-circuits problem behavior before it reaches his door. "People will tell you," he notes, "that the best—and worst—thing about living in a small town is that everyone knows everybody else's business. It's pretty hard for a kid to do something he shouldn't without it quickly becoming common knowledge."

Now in his second three-year term as a member of the school board, Harlin views the activities offered by the school and the genuine care of teachers like his mother as the reason the juvenile crime rate in Penelope is nonexistent. "Mom spends more time at school than she does at home," he says. "Last year, for instance, she tutored fourteen kids she took to the district literary competition." Pausing for emphasis, he then boasts, "All fourteen of them qualified to advance to regional."

7

W HAT WITH CLASSES, VOLLEYBALL PRACTICE, AND HOME-
work, Audra Osborne had been too busy during the
week to linger on the fact she had been selected as one of
the three finalists for the annual honor of Homecoming
Queen. Nor, for that matter, was she that excited about the
full-length red gown she would wear at the halftime ceremony Friday night. Karen Osborne had found it two years
earlier on a shopping trip to Waco, a $150 dress on sale for
just $20, and although her daughter had argued that she
had absolutely no need for such formal wear, the prudent
mom had purchased it anyway.

"You never know," she had suggested.

There is an almost carbon-copy likeness in the mother
and daughter, who have both spent their entire lives in
Penelope. Karen, one of thirteen students who graduated

in the class of 1977, had been a member of the school volleyball and basketball teams; she had also performed in the
one-act play ensemble that won the state championship in
her junior year and finished second when she was a senior.
She'd also graduated as the class valedictorian.

Now a member of the school board, a volunteer worker
in the concession stand on game nights, and a designated
organizer of class reunions, she can point not only to the
fact it is on land formerly owned by her father that the football field was built but that her mother continues to serve
as the elementary school librarian, a position she's held
since Karen was a youngster.

Audra has clearly followed in her mother's footsteps. In
addition to participating in athletics and acting yearly in the
school play, she is high among those currently in the running for the honor of valedictorian.

There are, however, differences in the mother-daughter
comparison. Karen, raised in a far stricter household than
the one she and husband Ronny now watch over, was not
allowed to be a cheerleader since her father had not looked
kindly on young girls wearing short dresses that showed too
much bare leg. Also, with no football team during the time
Karen had attended Penelope High, there had been no cel-
ebrations of Homecoming, and thus no Homecoming
Queen honor to be bestowed.

Still, although Karen, today a computer programmer-
analyst for a Waco firm, privately hoped that it would be

her daughter's name called out on Friday night, she was pleased that Audra was not viewing the coming coronation as a life-and-death matter. Ronny Osborne, meanwhile, was proud that his daughter was a queen candidate but was admittedly more concerned about the outcome of the game. A better-than-average player himself during his school days at Reicher High School in Waco, he was closely following the progress of son Ethan, a freshman end for the Wolverines.

As game day neared, Ethan's chief concern was how much playing time he might get. His sister's worry, meanwhile, was how she would juggle her responsibilities as a cheerleader with preparation for the halftime activities where she, Samantha Machac, or Tiffany Svacina would be crowned queen.

Finally, her mother had suggested that since there would be little time to change from her cheerleader uniform into her dress once the game was under way, it was best that she put off cheerleading until the second half.

What neither of the women knew was that the Wolverine coaches were hoping there would be no need for cheering past halftime. If Willie Harlin's scouting report was accurate, the team not only had every opportunity to win but might well accomplish the first mercy-rule victory in the school's young football history.

The Penelope players were already gathered outside the dressing room when the Faith Family Academy team arrived, not in the traditional yellow school bus favored by most schools, but in a small caravan of minivans. The eighteen visiting players who piled out, already in uniform, represented the small charter school's first-ever attempt at competitive athletics. Even to the winless Wolverines, they looked several degrees shy of a formidable opponent.

From the opening kickoff it was obvious that the young players from Waxahachie, disorganized and clearly intimidated, were vastly overmatched. And as they regularly missed assignments, dropped passes, failed to make tackles, and blocked poorly, if at all, a steady chorus of criticism began ringing out from the small gathering of parents and fellow students who had followed the team to Penelope ("Dammit, you guys get back out there and knock somebody on his butt," one father urged). April McAdams listened and slowly shook her head. "That," she whispered as she looked toward the opposite sideline, "was us a couple of years ago."

Penelope scored easily and often. Lozano raced untouched for three touchdowns in the first quarter alone. McCabe connected on a pass to Rendon for another.

With over seven minutes left to play in the half, McCabe had thrown two more touchdown passes, another to Rendon and one to freshman Jonathan Moreno. Minutes later Lozano ran for another; then, with just over a minute left in the half, he raced seventy yards for another touchdown that brought the score to 59–0.

And in less than twenty minutes of playing time, it was over, destined to be forever remembered as the victory that had ended the long drought and established a lengthy list of new school records—most points scored and first-ever shutout, among others. Yet even the winners, coaches and players alike, acknowledged that the long-awaited success had come far too easily.

As several Penelope fans approached Kyle McCabe to offer congratulations, he smiled and quickly put things into perspective. It felt great to finally win, he admitted, but "it will feel even better when we beat a really good team."

All that remained was a halftime show that had suddenly been turned into a postgame event.

Little girls, dressed in school colors and wearing the traditional Homecoming mums, watched in envy as the high school royalty assembled on the sidelines to be introduced. Keeping with tradition, senior members of the team would escort the queen candidates onto the field.

All that was missing was the familiar voice of Mike Baker. The teacher–public address announcer was in the unique situation of being not only a member of the Penelope High faculty but also serving on the school board in Hubbard. In the latter capacity he had been called away to a weekend seminar in Dallas and had yielded his announcing duties to basketball coach Harley Davis.

First, the underclass princesses, serving as the court for the senior Homecoming Queen candidates, slowly marched onto the field. Freshman Jaimee Erskine, escorted by classmate Jonathan Moreno, shyly smiled as those in the stands applauded. Then came sophomore princess Sherry Rendon, accompanied by Ben Patrick. Mason Ewell escorted junior class princess Lauren Watson.

"And now," Davis dramatically informed the crowd, "the candidates for this year's Homecoming Queen."

I stood to one side, amazed at the transition that was playing out before me. Young girls I'd seen daily in jeans and running shoes, or dressed for volleyball practice, had suddenly become attractive young women, hair styled, faces aglow.

Kyle McCabe, looking embarrassed, had Tiffany Svacina on his arm. Next came Audra and Michael Lozano. Then Samantha Machac, accompanied by Joe Rendon.

As they stood there, frozen in a moment that would provide them with fond memories for a lifetime, cheers and applause echoed into the night air.

"The 2004 Penelope High School Homecoming Queen," Davis then announced, "is . . . Miss Audra Nicole Osborne."

In the stands, Karen Osborne, having left the concession stand to view the ceremony, briefly put her hands to her face, then turned to tearfully embrace her husband. On the field, Natalie Matula, the previous year's queen, having returned from college to participate in the ceremony, passed her title along to the new honoree.

A new chapter had been added to the Osborne family legacy.

———

Celebration of the Homecoming Queen ceremony and the milestone victory would be brief. Yearbook sponsor Kim Quiram, previously busy taking pictures of the Homecoming activities, rushed to get a photograph of the scoreboard before its lights were switched off. Karen Osborne, camera in hand, insisted that son Ethan pose with his newly crowned sister before leaving the field. In less than a half hour after the ceremony, the stands and parking lot were deserted.

Audra had returned home to change into jeans and a sweatshirt and play video games, her tiara casually perched atop her computer. Michael Lozano and girlfriend Daisy Pineda slowly walked hand in hand along the dirt road that led to the Lozano home. Kyle McCabe was invited to spend the weekend with friend Mason Ewell. They planned a night watching a couple of rented football movies: *Varsity Blues* and *The Program*. Out of the earshot of adults, a few of the students were organizing a "pasture party," where several pickups would gather in an isolated country spot, and the kids would blast their music into the night air and consume a few beers.

Long after everyone else had gone, the coaches lingered in their small office to watch the film of the game, savoring their first victory. "The kids needed this so badly," McAdams said. "If you don't ever win, it just gets too hard, too discouraging." Ballew agreed. Each was pleased that every player on the team had gotten into the abbreviated game. "You know what impressed me?" said Bellows. "All this time, waiting to get a win, I've wondered how they would react." They had done so, he proudly observed, with a great deal of grace.

It was almost midnight when McAdams finally telephoned his mom and dad to pass along the good news.

Cheerleader Lauren Watson, meanwhile, had returned home to write a lengthy e-mail message to former Penelope student Jason Atkins, sharing news of the team's victory and details of the Homecoming activities.

Thousands of miles away, where he was stationed in the highly volatile Iraqi city of Fallujah, Marine Lance Corporal Atkins was Penelope's lone participant in the war against terrorism.

8

I LEARNED QUICKLY AS I BEGAN MY VISITS TO PENELOPE THAT things are not always as they seem. It had been back in the early days of August, when I'd stopped by one afternoon to watch as the team went through one of its initial practices, that I'd first seen Jason Atkins.

As the young players, dressed in full football gear, began doing wind sprints, there he was, in jeans, wearing neither shirt nor shoes, happily sprinting alongside the players. And immediately my thoughts returned to so many past visits to small towns where I'd met countless young men, aimlessly locked into the wonder years of high school athletics. I'd seen them on the town squares, still proudly wearing their letter jackets years after graduation and met them in the stands at more schoolboy games than I can remember, listening as they talked wistfully of past Friday night feats as if they had occurred only yesterday. They were their towns' by-gone heroes, unable to let go of what had been—and, per-haps, would forever be—the greatest moments of their lives.

That, I immediately assumed, was the sad story of the stranger visiting the Wolverines practice. Clearly older than those in uniform, he happily raced to the lead of each up-and-down-the-field run. Taking note of the tolerance shown by the coaches, I assumed he had once played for Penelope.

On that count, at least, I was right.

When the team took a brief water break, I approached Coach Bellows and nodded in the direction of the inter-loper. "Who the hell's that?" I asked.

"Jason Atkins," the assistant coach said. "He's in the Marines, home on leave from Camp Pendleton and just try-ing to stay in shape. He's shipping out to Iraq next week." Until that moment, it had not occurred to me that even our nation's rural waystops, the tiny and isolated communities far removed from so much of the world's day-in, day-out in-sanity, were also sending their children off to battle. "He's a really good kid. Played ball for us," Bellows said, "and was valedictorian his senior year."

"How old is he?"

"Nineteen."

Keeping my earlier misconceptions to myself, I had asked that Bellows introduce me to Atkins once practice was over. "I want to shake his hand," I said.

Now, as the days of September are fading, Veda Atkins, teacher of English and special education at Penelope, never sleeps before praying for the safety of the grandson she has raised since he was two. It has become her early morning ritual to monitor several cable stations for news of the war before leaving home for her classroom.

And it pleased her to know that Lauren Watson was keeping Jason updated on what was happening back home.

As she sat in her class, awaiting the beginning of a new school day, Atkins made no attempt to hide the fact that she is constantly worried. Jason's infrequent calls to her and her surveyor husband bring brief and welcome relief, but little insight into what he's doing or how he's coping with life as a soldier. "He never really says much. I can only guess that maybe he isn't allowed to tell us where he is or anything about what he's doing," she surmises.

"But, then," she adds, "the truth is, he's never been very good about letting you know what's going on." Smiling, she recounts his frustrating search for a job following graduation. For several weeks he'd knocked on doors and filled out applications in Waco and Hillsboro with no success. "Then, one day he came home all smiles and said, 'Well, I finally got a job. But it's going to involve a considerable amount of travel.' When I asked what he was going to do, he said, 'I've enlisted in the Marines.'"

Although she had no idea what battlefield her grandson might be fighting on, she was certain of one thing. "I can promise you," she says, "it gave him a really big lift when he heard from Lauren that the football team finally won a game."

Jason Atkins wasn't the only one. Even before Corey and April arrived at school on Monday morning, a floral arrangement had been delivered to Harley Johnson's office. Accompanying it was a card from Royce McAdams, addressed to his son and members of the team. "Congratulations," it read, "I knew you could do it."

Still, by the time the players reported for practice on Monday, the coaches had dismissed all thoughts of their historic victory. On the coming Friday night they would face an undefeated team that was the odds-on favorite to win the District 15 championship. Aquilla High, even with its all-state running back out with a shoulder injury, had defeated Morgan 50–0 the previous week and advanced to number nine in the state's six-man rankings.

Over the weekend, Coach Ballew had spoken with several coaching friends who had seen and been impressed by the Aquilla team. McAdams, meanwhile, had reviewed Willie Harlin's scouting report. "This," Ballew observed, "is a team that can kick our butts good if we're not ready to play."

"In that case," McAdams replied, "we'd better get ready."

While the team practiced, I watched for a time, enjoying the warm afternoon, then returned to the school in search of a woman whose efforts had, for years, helped earn Penelope High a reputation in the competitive arena that far exceeded anything the athletic program has ever accomplished. Annually, Gloria Walton oversees the productions of one-act plays that are the constant envy of schools far larger and better funded.

At last count, only six Texas high schools have won more state championships in one-act-play competitions than student thespians from Penelope.

It did not surprise me, then, to find her still at her desk long after her day's responsibilities as the school district's business manager had been completed. As she does during each fall semester, she was reading one of several plays stacked on the corner of her desk, trying to determine which she will choose to have the students perform in the spring.

The tradition she had inherited began back in the '70s, when her daughter, Pam, was a student actress directed by teacher Janice Trompler. During the six years Trompler was in charge of preparing students for the spring competition, her performers won the state championship twice and finished second in another year. Gloria, whose husband owned and operated the local granary, had volunteered to aid with costuming, makeup, and hairstyling.

When, in 1980, the business manager job at the school opened, Walton had moved from her desk at the granary into a small office next door to that of superintendent Johnson. And in addition to keeping track of the school's finances and helping to establish budgets, she has, for the past twenty-one years, organized and directed the school's plays.

"It gets in your blood," she confesses, her memory of past plays and performers remarkable. There was, for instance, the '93 streamlined adaptation of *Bus Stop*, which earned second place at the state finals. That year student Matt Beseda, whom she'd had difficulty persuading to try out, was recognized by state judges as Best Actor. The cast of the state qualifying *The Man Who Came to Dinner*, she admits, remains one of her favorites. And naturally, there are the disappointments. Although Penelope had won the district championship with the French farce *Widget Worries* several years ago, Walton had been dismayed that the judges had not seen fit to advance it beyond the regional competition. With obvious pride, she traces the generations of Penelope students who have participated. Lu Ann Matula, who now works as Johnson's secretary, was a member of a state-championship-winning cast. As was her husband. And their daughter, Natalie, who graduated the year before, had received honorable mention for her performance at the state finals. And there was Karen Osborne, who had won the Samuel French Award, given annually to the most outstanding character portrayal during the state competition, and who had now passed her acting torch to daughter, Audra. Walton had been particularly pleased when Mario Herrera, the center on Penelope's winless football team of 2003, was awarded a drama scholarship to Lon Morris College in Jacksonville, Texas.

Such a proud history has been accomplished on what is best described as a beg-and-borrow budget. The Penelope school does not even have a stage upon which the actors can practice or perform. Instead, they rehearse on the gymnasium floor. Costumes are sewn by mothers or scrounged from big-city thrift shops; props are loaned by people in the community. When the highly anticipated time comes each spring to put on the play for the student body and townspeople, it is performed in the school cafeteria.

"What we do have," says Walton, "are talented and dedicated kids. And a great deal of support from parents who understand why they have to be back at school to rehearse four nights a week once we get the cast and crew selected."

I found it remarkable that this woman, with no background in either drama or teaching, no acting career of her own from which to draw, had guided such uncommon success.

Walton grew up in Pidcoke, Texas, a community even smaller than Penelope, the daughter of an auto mechanic. She'd been married young to the manager of a series of small-town cotton gins. When, in 1971, her husband, Meredith, learned that the owner of the Penelope granary was retiring, he purchased it, and he and Gloria moved to the rolling landscape of Hill County.

Then, in '87, following a decade-long battle with multiple sclerosis, he died, leaving friends to wonder what the widowed Gloria might do. By then, she had fallen in love with Penelope, its people, and its gentle, easy ways. "I think," she says, "some were surprised when I told them I was going to stay right here and run my husband's business."

Today, the Walton Granary, the last surviving business in Penelope, still owned and operated by Gloria Walton, is the annual fall destination of the wheat, milo, and corn crops raised by neighboring farmers.

———————

If anyone can fully understand Walton's decision to remain in Penelope, it is Jan DeLapi, who assists her during the harvest season, weighing the truckloads of arriving grain and helping with bookkeeping chores. When not doing that, Jan, one of eight in the Penelope High graduating class of 1963, works in the school cafeteria. She also serves as the Penelope correspondent for the weekly newspapers in West and Hubbard.

She is one of those who long ago had taken leave of the region in which she was raised and ventured far into the world beyond before willingly acknowledging the call back home, to roots planted far deeper than she'd imagined.

DeLapi had been a cheerleader in the earlier days when Penelope had given football its first disastrous try, completing her senior year at the top of her class. She'd attended the University of Texas at Arlington, then married a manufacturing manager for Texas Instruments. Her husband's work had taken the couple to such widespread destinations as San Salvador, El Salvador, and Naples, Italy, and major cities throughout the United States before they divorced. For five years thereafter Jan had continued her world travels as a flight attendant for American Airlines before remarrying.

It was shortly after that she received word that her mother, still living near Penelope in the cotton gin community of Birone, was seriously ill. Jan and her new husband, a traveling produce-route manager for a Houston-based firm, bought a house just across the street from Jan's mother. In addition to making it possible for Jan to look after her mother, the move provided what she and her husband felt was a much needed new environment for their daughter, who had been faring poorly in the Houston school system.

"I had warned her," Jan recalls, "that life would be different here, that she would be attending a school where the students might not be as 'sophisticated' as some she'd known. But they were like a big family. All she needed to do to be accepted was reach out." The teenager, preparing to enter her freshman year, had initially fought against the move, angrily promising she would like neither the school nor its "country hick" students.

"But a couple of months into the school year," her mother remembers, "she came to her father and me and thanked us for making the move."

Soon, however, a series of family tragedies occurred. First, Jan's mother passed away. Then, suddenly, her brother. And finally, in 2000, after the discovery of an inoperable brain tumor, her husband died.

And in dealing with the losses, Jan determined that her place would never again be in the urban world. "When my husband was too sick to even get out of bed and I was working part time for Gloria and at the Birone cotton gin, I'd come home to find that someone had mowed the yard or left a fresh-baked pie on the kitchen table. If I needed help, I never had to ask for it.

"I had a healing process to get through," she now admits, "but I knew I was home, never again to leave."

Today, she cherishes the reborn friendships with old school classmates, the students who daily move through her cafeteria serving line, and her involvement in the community. Though a Baptist, she had been on hand the previous weekend to help out at the Catholic church's annual bazaar, serving the barbecue cooked by male members of the congregation, mingling with those who had come to wander among the displays of handmade quilts being auctioned off, watching the children as they played games of horseshoes while their parents played bingo and danced to the music of a polka band.

She and Gloria Walton, it occurred to me, are in a way kindred spirits: one daily providing students her made-from-scratch rolls and cobblers, the other offering them an opportunity to perform on a stage many had never even known existed before her gentle urgings.

————

Returning to the practice field, I watched as the players, tired and sweating, their helmets dangling at their sides, slowly made their way up the incline to the locker room. Had I not been on hand the previous spring to watch them in their roles in *The Secret Affairs of Mildred Wild,* it might never have occurred to me that quarterback Kyle McCabe and center Mason Ewell had talents that shone far beyond the athletic field.

And I wondered if, once they reached their adult years, they might be lured away by the glitter and promise of the big city or remain in the quiet comfort of the place they now called home. If the latter should be the case, I could not fault them.

9

ACHECKERBOARD OF BLACKTOP FARM ROADS WINDS THROUGH the southern edge of Hill County, past sandy-loam peanut farms and along the banks of the lazily flowing Brazos River, leading to the small town of Aquilla. No one, locals like to joke, arrives there by accident; you have to be looking for it. Like Penelope, it exists only because the school remains open despite two decades of rumors that closing and consolidation are just around the corner. Yet each fall, with the beginning of a new football season, the 138 residents are reminded why they continue their fight to survive. For years the farm boys who report to Coach Benny Weaver's opening practice do so in full knowledge that they are duty bound to uphold a long and proud tradition.

The Aquilla High Cougars, perennially a six-man football powerhouse, give the community not only life but bragging rights. And since that day a month earlier when they'd successfully opened their season in Hico on Six-Man Super Saturday, they had remained undefeated and steadily moving up in the statewide rankings. Despite tragedy and injury.

On the day Penelope was to visit, the Cougars pregame pep rally had taken a somber turn when, for the first time in the school's athletic history, a player's jersey was retired. In the spring, nineteen-year-old Canaan Ball, formerly an outstanding Aquilla player, had died in an automobile accident. Only a year earlier, his older brother, Dewayne, had lost his life when a four-wheeler he'd been riding in overturned.

It was time, Coach Weaver had decided, to extend formal condolences to the grief-ridden family. Standing with his team before the crowd that had assembled in the school's gymnasium, he solemnly announced that orange jersey Number 13, worn by Canaan Ball throughout his playing days, would be placed in the school's trophy case, the number never again to be assigned another Cougar player.

At the announcement, senior Josh Ball approached the coach to acknowledge the honor bestowed on his late brother. Limping noticeably on a foot that he had injured the previous week, the all-state center would not be able to play against the Wolverines.

Neither would the Cougars' talented running back Andrew Urbanovsky, who had been selected by the *Waco Tribune Herald* as the region's Six-Man Player of the Year at the end of the previous season. Having dislocated a shoulder, he was likely to miss the remainder of the season.

Among those disappointed that Urbanovsky would not be in uniform was Michael Lozano. Weekly, the Penelope running back had looked forward to the Tuesday edition of the Waco newspaper, turning quickly to the sports section, where the statistical leaders of teams in its circulation area were listed. On the week he and the Wolverines were due to travel to Aquilla, Lozano held a slight lead over Urbanovsky in total rushing yardage (895 to 839) after five games, and the Cougar back led in scoring (114 points to 84).

It pleased Corey McAdams that Lozano had looked forward to the challenge of proving himself in a head-to-head meeting with the celebrated Aquilla running back. The competitive flame the coach had so long been trying to ignite among his players had, he felt, finally begun to glow. At least in some.

But, obviously, not all.

Prior to a midweek practice, Randall Ballew entered the small coaches' office in the gym to find a note on his desk. "Coach Blu," it read, "I quit." It was signed by Ben Patrick.

All arms and legs, the gangly Patrick had, from the first day of practice, displayed remarkable coordination and shown absolutely no fear during tackling drills. His shoulder pads looked several sizes too large, sitting atop his 155-pound frame. There was something in his ever-present mischievous look that the coaches admired. On the other hand, it was a look that signaled the possibility that the new transfer might offer problems they would constantly be forced to address.

One afternoon following practice, Coach Ballew had passed the open door of the dressing room and overheard several of the players talking about the "jerk" who had joined the team. All efforts to help him fit in had failed, and they were pondering whether the problem should be taken to the coaches. "Naw," Ballew had heard someone say, "he's on our team now, he's one of us. We've just got to figure out a way to get him to straighten up and quit being such an asshole."

Finally, though, seniors Kyle McCabe and Michael Lozano had decided to go to the coaches for advice. After hearing their concerns, it was Ballew who suggested a solution. "What's important," he told the team captains, "is that everybody is on the same page. If one person's screwing it up for everyone else, making it difficult for us to accomplish the things we want to, he's not welcome." The decision, he added, was up to the team. "The way I see it, you've got two choices: Do everything you can to help him get his act together, make him feel like he's one of us. If you don't think that's going to work, just give Coach McAdams and me the word and we'll send him home."

The coaches were pleased when they heard that their players didn't want Patrick dismissed from the team. "We'll work it out," McCabe said.

"And we'll help," Ballew promised.

It had been McAdams who first recognized the real difficulty Patrick was experiencing: The youngster's self-esteem was virtually nonexistent, a problem often disguised by his overbearing behavior.

Early in the preseason practices, the coach glimpsed the problem. Following a late-afternoon workout, he had told members of the team to go to the elementary school gym, where a makeshift weight room had been set up. And although the others had gone directly to lift, Patrick, having no experience in athletics and unaware of the routine, had first gone to the dressing room and changed.

Seeing him arrive in the gym in jeans and T-shirt, McAdams had instructed him to go back and put on his uniform. "We don't lift weights in street clothes," he'd said.

Patrick, obviously embarrassed, turned and quickly left the gym. And when he hadn't returned in a reasonable amount of time, McAdams went looking for him. He found Ben seated on the curb of the school parking lot.

"What are you doing?" the coach asked.

Patrick shrugged. "I can't do this," he replied. "I can't do *nothing*." People, he said, had been telling him he was a "loser" for as long as he could remember. "And they were right. I don't want to play football."

Sitting beside the troubled teenager, McAdams spoke gently. "Look," he said, "I know moving to a new school is really hard. Right now you're feeling like you're never going to fit in. But if you're willing to do your part, to make the effort, it will happen. I promise you that. Ben, I know these kids; they'll give you every chance in the world if you'll just meet them halfway."

The sad-faced youngster only shook his head. Gone was the attitude, the quick and smart-mouthed response.

"So far as playing football," McAdams continued, "you've already shown me you can be one of the best players we've got. You would be making a big mistake to quit—on yourself or this team."

For several minutes the two sat in silence, Ben idly tossing pieces of gravel across the parking lot. Finally, he stood up and exhaled a weary sigh. "I'll go put my uniform back on," he said.

Patrick's problems, however, were too numerous to be solved by one conversation. Although his behavior on the football field improved, the classroom became a new battleground as soon as school opened. Almost daily, reports reached the office of principal Gordon Vogel or superin-

WHERE DREAMS DIE HARD | 107

tendent Johnson about Patrick's misbehavior, disruption of class, or refusal to turn in assignments.

By the time preliminary grade reports were sent out after the third week, he was not making a passing grade in any of his classes. Once the six-week report cards were issued, it was almost certain he would no longer be eligible to continue playing football.

The note left on Ballew's desk, then, had all the earmarks of a preemptive strike. "If we just let him quit," McAdams said, "I'm afraid we'll lose him for good." Ballew agreed.

Before the afternoon practice, the coach found Patrick in the gym and angrily motioned for him. "Get your ass into the locker room and get dressed for practice," Ballew demanded.

"Didn't you get my note?"

"I don't pay attention to notes."

"But, Coach, I quit football."

"You can do that—right after the season's over," the coach replied. "You started; you're going to finish. I'm going to see to that if I have to chase you all over town every afternoon."

There was only a feeble attempt to argue before Ballew continued. "Ben, I'm going to be real honest with you. This team doesn't need you all that much. We'd do fine without you. But what you don't seem to understand is that *you really need this team.*"

———

Among those who had looked forward to a Lozano-Urbanovsky matchup in Aquilla was Dr. Bob McCrummen, a retired university professor living in the Dallas suburb of Carrollton.

On the wall in his study is a large map of Texas, the location of each community where six-man football is played carefully circled. And for the past half dozen years, he and his wife, Mary, also a retired teacher, have made it their fall Friday ritual to travel to a six-man football game.

"Sometimes," McCrummen says, "we'll drive out Interstate 20 toward West Texas; sometimes we head south. We just look for what we think will be an exciting game at an interesting place, then check the map to see if there is a good restaurant somewhere along the way where we can stop to have an early dinner."

On this particular weekend, their destination was first a steakhouse on the outskirts of Waco and then the football stadium in Aquilla. Earlier in the day, they had telephoned the school, asking if their small pet pug, Molly, would be allowed into the game if kept on a leash.

The secretary who took the call had laughed as she admitted it was the first time she'd been asked the question. "Since I don't remember attending a Cougars game in the past fifteen years when there weren't at least a couple of stray dogs running around, sometimes out on the field during the game, I can't see why one on a leash can't come, too," she'd said.

And so it was that a friendly bark from Molly had drawn me to the couple soon after I arrived at the stadium. As the teams went through their warm-ups, Dr. McCrummen explained what beckons him and his wife to their weekly visits to the Texas heartland. "The games," he said, "are fun to watch, but truthfully, it is the atmosphere of these small towns that is so appealing. I love driving down their streets and having the townspeople wave and say hello. I love the community spirit you see in these little stadiums, the smell of the hamburgers and hotdogs cooking on the grills to be sold in the concession stand by members of the booster club, and the public address announcer's saying things like 'All students are welcome to the fifth-quarter gathering that will be held at the education building of the First Baptist Church immediately after the game.'"

"It's like stepping into a Norman Rockwell painting," his wife adds.

Like me, the McCrummens found something comforting, something reassuring, during their travels along the hidden country roads of the state.

It was almost time for the kickoff when Penelope cheer-leader sponsor Tinsley Olson pulled her van into the park-ing lot and the girls piled out and hurried toward the playing field. Audra Osborne and Lauren Watson had played in a volleyball game in Coolidge that had finished only an hour earlier. They had quickly showered and changed from their volleyball uniforms into their red-and-white cheerleading outfits.

As they made their way along the sideline, freshman player Chad Kerr shouted toward Lauren. "Ya'll win?"

The cheerleader flashed a smile and gave a thumbs-up. They had opened their district season with a victory. "Now," she shouted back, "it's you guys' turn."

If Aquilla was feeling the loss of its injured players, there was little evidence. The Cougars, in fact, took command of the game immediately, returning the opening kickoff for a touchdown. Briefly, however, it appeared the Wolverines would make a game of it. As his sister cheered, Ethan Os-borne made a circus catch of a Kyle McCabe pass, wrestling the ball away from a defender who briefly ap-peared to have made an interception; then Lozano made a couple of weaving runs for first downs. McAdams called the same Lozano-to-McCabe pass play that had been so successful the week before. Kyle made the catch and raced into the end zone to narrow Aquilla's advantage to 8–6. It was, however, as close as the Wolverines would get.

Overpowering the clearly outmanned Penelope squad, the Cougars scored on long runs, long passes, and an interception that was returned for a touchdown. A Penelope fumble set up an easy Aquilla score. By halftime, the Cougars led, 50–6.

For the first time since the season had begun, I was watching a group of players who were obviously intimidated by their opponent. Not only was Aquilla the better team, but the Wolverines had quickly resigned themselves to defeat. The "butt kicking" that Coach Ballew had warned about was well under way.

And it ended less than a minute into the third quarter. Aquilla recovered a fumble on the second half kickoff, then scored on its first play from scrimmage to advance the score to 56–6. For the first time of the season, Penelope had been "forty-five-pointed," a victim of the game's mercy rule.

The little town of Aquilla might be vanishing, but its football prowess was obviously alive and well.

On the ride home, Lozano, distressed over his fumble, which had set the stage for the opposition's final touchdown, sat alone, eyes shut, brooding. He could hear the laughter and joking of several of his teammates, and it made him angry. Among the loudest was Ben Patrick. He had clearly been the Wolverines' best defensive player, focused, aggressive, and on several occasions tackling Aquilla ball carriers for losses. Now, however, he was snidely remarking on the futility of continuing the season.

What was hidden beneath the flippant sarcasm was the knowledge he'd soon play his final game of the year. He knew that when report cards were issued in two weeks, he would no longer be eligible.

What Coach McAdams, seated next to his wife at the front of the bus, was feeling was a lingering sense of disappointment. Realistically, he had not expected his team to win, but he had believed they would play far better than they had. It was, he had frankly told the team as it had retreated to the dressing room, the worst game they had played all season. Several times during the short ride back to Penelope, he considered calming down the talk and laughter he heard behind him ("Back when I was playing, if you got beat, no one said a word on the ride home. Even if you weren't really upset by the loss, you made sure the coach thought you were"), but he ultimately decided against it.

April reached across to squeeze his hand. "What it boils down to," he whispered to her, "is the fact we have some kids who are willing to put their hearts into what we're trying to do—and some who never will."

10

HARLEY JOHNSON HAD SPENT THREE DECADES IN EDUCATION, the last thirteen years as an administrator in the nearby Abbott school system before retirement had finally beckoned. His last professional function, he'd decided, would be to acknowledge the request of the neighboring Penelope school board members who had sought his expertise as they searched for a new superintendent. Asked to evaluate each applicant, Johnson had spent a good deal of time at the school in the spring of 1999, getting to know the teachers, meeting students, and sitting in on interviews with candidates for the vacant job. Quickly, he came to admire the dedicated approach of Penelope teachers and was impressed by the fact that serious discipline problems among the students were all but nonexistent. Also, he had liked the attitude of the townspeople and their quiet understanding that if their tiny community was to survive, support of the school was first and foremost.

Eventually, the white-bearded Johnson had confided to his wife that he'd become fascinated by the little Hill County school and was seriously thinking of postponing his retirement plans and adding his own name to the list of applicants. The watercolor painting and writing of occasional op-ed columns for the Waco newspaper that had become his leisure passions could wait a bit longer.

That summer he was unanimously selected as the new superintendent of the Penelope Independent School District (ISD). It is, he now admits, the most rewarding job he's ever held.

One midweek afternoon as we sat in his office long after the school day had ended, I asked what keeps him in a position that offers longer hours and less pay than almost any other he'd worked in during his academic career.

Without hesitation he began to tell this story:

It had, he recalled, been during the spring semester the previous year when a shy sophomore student named Jordan Faulkner—a youngster who lived with his single mother in a house trailer across the street from the post office—sat in his office as a penalty for missing recent classes without an excused absence. Faulkner, not among the most popular kids in school, not a member of any of its athletic teams or a participant in any of its social activities, had said nothing as he slumped in a nearby chair, dutifully passing his detention time.

Then, a female student had breathlessly entered Johnson's office to tell him that there had been a terrible automobile accident on the outskirts of town. Seeing who was seated in the superintendent's office at the time, the girl stopped short of adding more detail.

Instructing Faulkner to stay put, Johnson had quickly driven to the site of the wreck and learned that the victim was the mother of the boy sitting back in his office. Seriously injured, she had been taken by ambulance to the hospital in Hillsboro.

"When I got back to the school and told Jordan that his mom had been in an accident, he just grinned, not really grasping the seriousness of the situation. He pointed out that his mother was a heavy drinker and that she'd had five or six car wrecks in the last few years alone," Johnson told me. "Only after I explained that she was seriously injured did he begin to show real concern."

What neither knew at the time was that Faulkner's mother had suffered cardiac arrest en route to the hospital and died before ever reaching the emergency room.

"I didn't really know what to do for the kid," the superintendent admitted. "Finally, I asked him if he had any relatives I could contact and he mentioned a couple of uncles but was hesitant to give me their names or phone numbers.

It was pretty obvious they weren't close. After a while, though, he gave me one's number and I called, got no answer, and left a voice mail message."

Meanwhile, as Johnson pondered what to do until the uncle got in touch, Carol Brown, the mother of Penelope student Kayla Tucker, soon arrived and volunteered to take Jordan to her home for the night.

There young Faulkner had remained until his uncle finally phoned and said he would immediately begin making arrangements for Jordan. Upset by the idea of the bereaved teenager being moved, the family that was caring for him sought temporary custody so that Jordan might at least complete the school year before his future was decided. A judge had quickly agreed to their request.

"That kind of generosity in itself was pretty amazing," Johnson continued, "but didn't compare to what I saw from the students. To the best of my knowledge, Jordan hadn't had a friend in the world before this happened. He would walk to school alone every morning, head down, a hood usually pulled over his face. But when he lost his mother, the kids immediately rallied to his side. They offered him support, let him know he had friends, people who cared about him."

Several students, including Michael Lozano, had gone out to the home of the family with whom Jordan was temporarily living, just to talk.

When time came for the funeral, dozens of Penelope students and many of the teachers made the drive to Waco to attend.

As they arrived, the teenagers took seats toward the back of the chapel to somberly await the service. For most, it was the first experience with death and the protocol of a memorial.

"The first couple of rows are traditionally reserved for members of the deceased's family," Johnson said. "And Jordan was up there, sitting all alone. Until something remarkable began to happen."

One by one, fellow students left their places to quietly move down to the front rows and join him. As recorded hymns played and the scent of floral arrangements wafted through the room, the seats reserved for family were soon filled.

"It's things like that," says Johnson, "that keep me here."

There is also the daily challenge of maintaining high scholastic standards on Penelope's shoestring budget.

As Friday's game against rival Bynum approached, Johnson's apprehension had nothing to do with whether the football team might earn its second win of the season. Rather, he was worried about an announcement that was soon to be made by the Texas Education Agency.

Under President George W. Bush's No Child Left Behind initiative, which was designed to improve the quality of education nationwide, a rating system, based on a demanding variety of academic standards, had been established. To meet what was being called the Adequate Yearly Progress standard, students were required to score well on a variety of reading and math exams. Those schools that fared poorly would be designated Low Performing and not only face academic sanctions and embarrassment but the possible loss of students. Under the new guidelines, if a school was judged substandard, any of its students were eligible to immediately transfer to another, higher-performing school of their choosing.

Johnson did not want his school judged below par, nor did he wish to lose any of the 183 students who populated his combined elementary, junior high, and high school.

Though confident in his teaching staff, he was keenly aware of the shortfalls that they faced daily. Most, he knew, routinely bought necessary classroom supplies from their own pockets. Of Penelope's students, 77 percent were from economically disadvantaged homes. And in recent years, the steady arrival of new Hispanic families lured to small-town life had decidedly increased the number of students with limited English language skills. The Penelope school district had, since Johnson's arrival, remained among the poorest in the state of Texas.

The district covers only 48.6 square miles and is mostly farm and pasture land with a total tax value of less than $14 million. In addition to the low tax base of the community, Penelope could not, as could many public schools, anticipate substantial donations from wealthy benefactors.

The state funding that the school annually receives is based on the average daily attendance. Were attendance to decrease dramatically, the stipend was likely to be reduced or even completely cut off, with a strongly worded suggestion that Penelope students might be better served if they were included in a consolidation program with a neighboring school.

For Johnson, it is a constant fear, a challenge he considers daily. Maintain a high level of academic performance among the students or their parents are likely—and justifiably—to opt to have them travel to Hubbard or West, to Malone or Bynum or Mount Calm for their education. And should such an unthinkable event occur, the hundred-year-old school might cease to exist.

It is just such a catastrophe that Johnson has pledged to guard against. Aware that his curriculum doesn't compare to those in larger schools, he innovates. Thanks to the arrival of the computer age, Penelope students can now even take interactive college courses. He points to their unique opportunity to participate in virtually every school-related activity they choose, so long as they are academically eligible. No one is denied a spot on the athletic teams. And while there are tryouts by which cheerleaders are selected, if one wants to be a member of the squad, none who are academically eligible are turned away.

In such an environment, the dropout rate has been minimal at Penelope; the graduation rate has, for the past several years, been 100 percent.

Still, the superintendent was relieved when the fax machine in his office finally delivered the good news that the Penelope ISD had received a passing grade from the state educational authorities.

Over two hundred schools in Texas, many of them far larger and more solvent than Penelope, had not been so fortunate and had been assigned substandard ratings.

11

IN HILL COUNTY, THE GEOGRAPHY DICTATING EDUCATIONAL OP-
portunities is not easy to chart. In Malone, just eight
miles up Farm Road 308 from Penelope, the school serves
its seventy youngsters only until they reach the eighth
grade. Thus, for their high school years, the students have
the choice to attend school in either Hubbard, Penelope, or
Bynum. To the east, the little community of Mount Calm
offers a similar choice to its students after they have completed junior high: They can travel to Hubbard, Axtell, or
Penelope. In what is best described as an academic game
of hopscotch, even a few Hillsboro kids are allowed to attend school in Bynum.

Competition among the schools for the young transfers
is fierce, inasmuch as each new face adds to the ever-
important Average Daily Attendance figures that determine

school funding. Still, so far as Harley Johnson knew, recruiting of athletes by rival schools had never been an issue of any concern.

Then, as the new school year approached, came talk that Penelope might be in danger of losing some of its student athletes to Bynum. There was no real evidence, just rumors, and Johnson initially assumed that the matter was a product of frivolous small-town gossip. Penelope, after all, hardly had the reputation of churning out superstar players coveted by others.

But just days before the beginning of the fall semester a fax from the Bynum school arrived in the superintendent's office, requesting the results of sophomore Josh Baumgardner's pre–football season physical exam. A standout player for Coach McAdams the previous fall, an all-district selection in basketball, and the Penelope High freshman class favorite, Baumgardner was, in fact, moving to Bynum. His mother confirmed the disappointing news when she arrived at the Penelope school to withdraw her son, explaining that she had just purchased a home in the nearby community.

Thus Johnson decided to voice his growing concern during the annual August pre-school meeting of district officials held at the Lone Star Café in Hillsboro. Fearing that the rules of fair play might have been violated, he informed the gathering that when he filled out the required transfer paperwork he would indicate that young Baumgardner was making the move "for athletic reasons." A tempest briefly bubbled as the District 15-A executive committee agreed to look into the matter. So did Bynum superintendent Polly Boyd.

The result of their findings: No district bylaws had been violated. They found no reason to believe there had been anything illegal about Baumgardner's transfer.

Sitting in his classroom one afternoon, Bynum coach Andy Ball, in his second year as the school's football coach, reflected on the late summer rumors the player had been illegally lured to his school and insisted they were without merit. He explained that he had not even been aware the Baumgardners were moving to Bynum until he learned they had purchased a house there. "I didn't recruit anyone," the thirty-six-year-old coach said. "I'm not going to jeopardize my career for some high school kid."

Thus ended the brief furor. But not Johnson's suspicion. Or the rivalry.

———

Much like Penelope, Bynum is a little town that has stubbornly refused to die. Established in 1882, it lost most of its business district in a 1925 fire. Then only five years later, just as rebuilding of the town had been completed and the life of the townspeople had returned to normal, a tornado swept through, causing extensive damage. Bynum rebuilt again and today clings to life, just as does Penelope.

Over the years, the closeness of the two communities has fueled a fierce rivalry, their schools' highly charged competitions long predating Penelope's return to football. Basketball battles between the boys' and girls' teams were legendary. And while neither had made much of a mark with their football teams—each would enter Friday's game with only one win—it was a given that an overflow crowd would be on hand when the Bynum Bulldogs traveled the eighteen miles to their meeting with the Wolverines.

The starting quarterback for the visitors would be sophomore Josh Baumgardner.

———

Coach Ballew, unfamiliar with the history of the Bynum-Penelope rivalry, had quickly sensed a different attitude among the players as they practiced during the week. It was obvious as he and the other coaches had gone over scouting reports, outlined the game plan, and hammered home their sincere belief that they would be the better team on the field Friday night. A win, the players were reminded, would be the first against a district opponent in Penelope's history.

"This," Ballew told McAdams and Bellows on Thursday, "reminds me of the feeling we used to get every year in Abbott before our big game against Aquilla. It's obvious this one is important to these kids; they really want to win it."

"They aren't the only ones," McAdams replied. The earlier win against Faith Family Academy had been a positive step, but no one on the team had sincerely believed they had achieved any real milestone with the lopsided victory. Defeating an equal, a district opponent, a longtime rival, would be the shot in the arm the coach desperately wanted for his players.

And it was obvious that the players were aware of the stakes as well. Lozano, held out of practice while the hamstring injury he'd suffered in the previous week's game healed, had secretly walked over to the darkened football field after dinner each evening and run countless wind sprints to make certain he would be ready to play.

Long before the kickoff the stands were filled, and fans stood shoulder-to-shoulder along the fences bordering the home and visitors' sides, ensuring the largest crowd ever assembled in the two-year-old stadium. Mason Ewell's electrician father, Paul, once an all-state pitcher with a wicked curve ball, had driven down from DeSoto and stood with Tracy Joslin, the youngster's stepfather. Paul Lozano had escorted Michael's grandmother to a spot in the stands before finding his place at the fence.

And the game quickly lived up to expectations. The aggressive defensive game plan Ballew had designed confused young Baumgardner and the Bynum offense. Penelope,

meanwhile, was also finding the going tough as Kyle Mc-
Cabe and Michael Lozano were regularly thrown for losses.
At the end of the first quarter, the score was an unlikely
0–0.

"Coach," Ballew whispered to McAdams on the sidelines, "we've got 'em on their heels." Bynum, he suggested,
hadn't been ready for the kind of determined effort it was
seeing from Penelope's players.

Early in the second quarter, however, the Bulldogs
ended a lengthy drive with a one-yard touchdown run by
senior Justin Duvall. Mason Ewell stood in the end zone,
fists clenched, and was yelling at his Wolverine teammates. "That's OK," he said. "We'll get it back. We'll get it
back."

And in less than three minutes they did. On a trick play
McAdams had designed earlier in the week. McCabe, having had difficulty getting his passes away against the charg-
ing Bynum defense, lateraled the ball to Lozano, feinted an
effort to block, then raced downfield on a pass pattern.
Lozano lofted the ball over the head of a defender, and Mc-
Cabe made the catch for the touchdown. When Lozano
threw to freshman end Chris Culpepper for the extra point,
Penelope was suddenly in the lead, 7–6.

Then, with only a minute remaining in the half, Lozano,
showing no ill effects from the hamstring injury, outran the
Bynum defense to score and then threw a pass to Ewell for
the extra point.

As the Wolverines made their way to the dressing room, leading 14–6, Ballew stopped briefly to shake hands with Lozano's dad. He leaned close to the obviously pleased father. "I'm seeing something in their eyes tonight that hasn't been there all year," the coach whispered.

In the third quarter, however, it became obvious why Josh Baumgardner had been welcomed to his new home. With two quick touchdown passes against his former teammates, he put Bynum back into the lead.

But in short order, McCabe responded. On a fourth down with just three minutes remaining in the quarter, he connected with Josh Hampton for a touchdown that put the Wolverines ahead. Lozano kicked the two-point conversion that improved the slim margin to 22–18.

In the final hectic minutes of the third quarter, though, Baumgardner threw his third touchdown pass of the night; then Brandon Mobley brought the Bynum fans to their feet with a sixty-yard run for another score. As the fourth quarter began, the Bulldogs had built a 33–22 lead.

Lozano narrowed the margin with a touchdown run with two minutes gone in the final quarter, but by then the players for both teams resembled punch-weary boxers. Exhausted, they battled each other to a standstill until 0:00 finally showed on the scoreboard clock. Bynum fans poured onto the field to congratulate their team on its 33–28 victory while Penelope supporters sat wilted in disappointment, quieted by the narrow defeat.

As the teams lined up for the traditional postgame handshakes, I was eager to see the response the Penelope players and coaches would have to Baumgardner. He had, it could be safely said, been the difference in the game. If there was any resentment over his leave-taking, I did not see it. Obviously no friendships had suffered irreparable damage. Corey McAdams shook the youngster's hand and praised his performance. So did Ballew and Bellows.

At the far end of the field, however, Harley Johnson still stood where he'd kept his traditional vigil by the end zone fence that guarded the Domesle brothers' pasture. Clearly disappointed, he was in no mood to offer congratulations.

———

April McAdams had never seen her husband so painfully despondent over a loss. Throughout the weekend he replayed the game in his head, pointing to crucial turns that could have changed its outcome, the plays he'd called, decisions he'd made that, in retrospect, he judged ill conceived. Regardless of the positives his wife pointed out as she went through her routine of recording the team's statistics, she was able to do little to lighten his mood. "We should have won," he repeatedly told her. "It was right there for us, right up until the last drive of the game."

April stopped short of reminding him that the game had served as proof of his father's observation: The most difficult job in coaching is teaching kids how to win, even when they have that opportunity.

By Monday morning, Corey McAdams had vowed not to allow his players to share his lingering disappointment. There was another game to prepare for. What the young coach privately feared, however, was that the enthusiasm for the season might now be gone, forever stolen away by the missed chance at victory.

In the days to come, that fear would be painfully realized.

12

As a sportswriter covering football at all levels from high school to the NFL, I had learned that the dynamic of a coaching staff, regardless of its size, is a major factor in the progress and success of any team. A well-defined division of responsibilities, the sharing of ideas and strategies, and the opportunity to teach myriad aspects of the game simultaneously during a single practice are invaluable.

During his first two years as Penelope's head coach, Corey McAdams had been assisted by Charles Bellows and Phillip Esparza, fellow teachers eager to help but admittedly limited in football knowledge. Virtually all of the technical aspects of the game—from pass routes and blocking assignments on offense to tackling techniques on defense—were taught by the overburdened McAdams. Rarely when a practice ended did he feel that everything his team needed to work on had been addressed.

Then, when Esparza and his wife began building a new home just a few blocks from the school, he had understandably begged off the responsibilities of coaching. And though Bellows continued to report for practices following long days of teaching junior high science, it was increasingly obvious that McAdams was sorely in need of help.

It had come unexpectedly.

The previous spring, Michele Kreder and her husband were visiting with longtime friends Randall and Annette Ballew, when Randall casually asked the volleyball coach if there were any openings for teachers at her school. Michele had, at first, dismissed the question, certain that Randall, one of the most respected coaches in the Abbott school system, would never make the eleven-mile move to a school whose football program was both winless and doomed to endless struggle.

As an assistant for six years, he had been a key part of Abbott's perennial success. The Panthers had won district in 1999, gone to the state quarterfinals in 2000 before losing to eventual state champion Panther Creek, and in 2002 they had reached the semifinals, where they were finally defeated by Calvert, which had also gone on to win the state title. Energetic and outgoing, Ballew was not only a favorite of Abbott players but also an exceptional classroom teacher.

There was, Kreder assumed, every reason in the world, short of a lucrative offer to become a head coach somewhere nearby, for Randall to remain in Abbott. He loved the little ten-acre farm on which he raised a few Black Angus cattle, and his roots in the community ran deep. His older sister, Doris Beseda, was the school's principal; his parents lived nearby. For years he'd half-joked to friends during morning coffee gatherings down at the Abbott Cash Grocery that when he died he'd like his tombstone to be placed in the front yard of his home on the outskirts of town.

It was with reservations, then, that Kreder approached Harley Johnson to suggest that an outstanding football coach had expressed interest in a job at Penelope.

"We've got a coach," Johnson replied, making clear that he was satisfied with McAdams's work.

"He's not asking about the head coaching job," Michelle replied. "He's interested in being Corey's assistant."

"What does he teach?"

"American and world history."

Johnson, who had briefly coached during the early days of his own education career, was convinced that McAdams had to eventually have an experienced assistant if his football program was ever to prosper. The superintendent, meanwhile, also needed to hire a history teacher before the new school year began. Reaching for a pencil, he said, "Give me his number."

At age thirty-four, Randall Ballew—a good-natured, firm-handshake type with an easy smile and the taut, compact frame of one who's done his share of heavy lifting—had never strayed far from the Central Texas region where he'd been raised. His eighty-year-old father, Randall, Sr., had served in World War II, then earned a law degree from Baylor University, only to decide belatedly that he preferred the outdoors and country living to the courtroom and the big-city rat race. Thus he had spent his entire life as a farmer, raising peanuts, cantaloupes, and watermelons in the sandy river-bottom land near rural Gholson. He and his wife had also raised six children, five daughters and Randall, their youngest.

The Gholson school system, like that in Malone, went only through the eighth grade, thus offering the youngest Ballew the option of attending whichever high school he wished. And since Connally High in nearby Waco had earned an impressive reputation as a producer of championship baseball teams, he'd opted to enroll there. Not only had the decision allowed him the opportunity to pursue his boyhood dream of one day becoming a big league catcher, but it was a choice of convenience. He could ride to school daily with another of his sisters, who worked there as a teacher.

Following graduation, he'd been determined to continue his baseball career at the collegiate level, making one-year, nonscholarship stops at Brownwood's Howard Payne University and then Dallas Baptist before the coach at East Texas Baptist in Marshall offered a grant-in-aid that would help finance the final two years of Randall's pursuit of a degree.

Briefly, in the mid-1990s, he'd taught and coached girls' athletics at the Connally Middle School but abruptly abandoned his teaching plans in favor of a better-paying career as a construction welder. Only when Abbott High School superintendent Terry Timmons phoned, offering an opportunity to resume teaching and coaching, did Randall's thoughts return to the classroom.

On three occasions, however, he turned the offer down, always pointing to the fact that his job in mobile home construction paid far better.

Timmons, however, had the right answer for Ballew's argument. He explained how his own teaching career had begun in nearby Penelope (where he'd even briefly directed the school's famed one-act plays). He'd thoroughly enjoyed his work but had eventually decided to leave education when offered a better-paying position as an executive in a fast-food chain. It had not taken him long, however, to realize that the increased income was no match for the satisfaction of teaching. Which, he explained, was why he'd decided to apply for an opening at Abbott High in hopes of returning to the challenge of teaching in a small school. He'd never regretted the decision, he said. Nor did he believe Ballew would.

Thus, in the fall of 1998, Randall Ballew put away his welding torch and returned to the academic world, this time with the added responsibility of assisting with the school's six-man football program. He'd quickly fallen in love with the reckless pace of the game. He loved coaching it and talking with others who coached it. He became a student of its history, watched endless hours of game films, and attended coaching schools to increase his knowledge. Although many he knew in the profession talked of one day making the jump to a larger school where the more traditional eleven-man game was played, Ballew was certain he would spend his coaching career at the six-man level. He enjoys being part of what he likes to refer to as "the six-man family."

And although after six years he had not yet been seriously bitten by the urge to advance to a head coaching position, he had become restless, feeling the need for a change. He had no intention of moving his family from Abbott but was ready to make a shift in his career. His wife, Annette, a certified public accountant for a Waco firm, urged him to follow his heart.

And by midsummer, he had agreed to become the new assistant football coach at Penelope. "You know," Annette warned, "there will be all kinds of rumors for a while." Indeed, in short order there was a suggestion that a rift with Abbott head coach Terry Crawford had resulted in Randall's decision to leave. Others surmised that Ballew had wearied of the unreasonable demands made by his principal-sister. Still others said they had heard that he'd been lured to Penelope by a sizable increase in salary and the promise that he would soon replace the winless McAdams as the school's head coach.

Although none of the speculations was true, it was only the last one that really concerned him. During preliminary talks about the opening with Harley Johnson, he had wanted it made clear to the current coach that he had no designs on his job. "You've got a good coach here," Ballew told the superintendent. "I'd just like the opportunity to help him however I can."

Far from feeling threatened, Corey McAdams was delighted by the news that help was on the way.

———

As I'd watched McAdams and Ballew on the practice field and in their classrooms, interacting with students and fellow teachers in the hallways, and listened as they discussed game plans, it occurred to me that they were young men ideally matched, opposite personalities that meshed perfectly in pursuit of their common goal. McAdams was quiet and reserved; Ballew was the outgoing, never-met-a-stranger type. Corey played the fatherly role well, offering quiet encouragement and understanding, soothing bruised egos. Ballew, although also positive and upbeat, could belt out the thunder and lightning when the need arose.

Charles Bellows, whom both had asked to continue as a member of the staff, agreed with my assessment. "I wouldn't have missed this for the world," he said one day as we stood watching practice. "These guys not only make a great team but are also fun to be around."

While spending time together at the summer coaching school in Lubbock, McAdams and Ballew had quickly agreed that Corey would coach the team's offense while Randall handled the defense. With this splitting of duties, they agreed, twice as much could be accomplished in each practice. As the season progressed, their plan was working. Though the season record might not show it, the kids were learning to play football.

———

During the week leading up to the team's visit to Abbott, McAdams had watched his assistant closely, saying little about it but keenly aware that the game against the players Ballew had once helped coach would be an emotional one. Randall, he knew, badly wanted to show friends there that he was helping bring a new enthusiasm to Penelope football.

Ballew, meanwhile, had said nothing of the ribbing he was receiving back home. Most had wished him well, but after an encounter with a longtime friend who warned him that the Panthers "were gonna score a hundred against that piss-ant little ol' team you're coaching," he'd decided it was best to avoid contact with people in the community in the remaining days leading up to the game.

"This," he'd confided to wife Annette, "isn't going to be easy."

Departure time had come, and McAdams was pacing the floor inside the school gym, his displeasure obvious. Outside, coaches Ballew and Bellows had already loaded the equipment and told the waiting players to get on the bus.

However, quarterback Kyle McCabe and center Mason Ewell had not arrived. They were among the most dependable members of the team, and their absence both worried and angered the coach. Then, just as he'd considered sending someone to see if there had been car problems or perhaps an accident, the two came running into the gym.

They were fifteen minutes late, their breathless explanation not one available to a city kid.

All week, Mason's stepfather had been telling him that a trailer load of goats would be arriving on Saturday and that it was his responsibility to see that a holding pen was built and ready. However, it had rained almost daily throughout the week, the weather providing an easy excuse for delaying the project. When Mason had arrived home from school on Friday afternoon, friend Kyle with him, Tracy Joslin was standing in the front yard. "You're not going anywhere," he firmly informed Mason, "until that pen is built."

Thus the two boys had worked frantically to complete the chore to Joslin's satisfaction before it was time to return to the school. Only when the final post had been set and the last strand of wire put in place did the secretly amused Joslin give an approving nod and send them on their way. "You boys get after 'em tonight," he called out. "We'll see you at the game."

"What are you going to do?" April whispered to her husband as they followed the tardy players to the waiting bus.

Corey finally smiled. "Hey," he shrugged, "when you've got a fence to build, you've gotta get it built, right?" His team, he added, needed no additional distractions.

Already, there had been too many. Sophomore end-linebacker Javier Marin had arrived at school with a note from his doctor, stating that the bruised ribs he'd suffered during the Bynum game had not properly healed, so he should not be allowed to play against Abbott. And the release of the first six-weeks report cards revealed that Ben Patrick had become academically ineligible and would not be making the trip.

And because of his ongoing discipline problems, principal Vogel had finally decreed that Patrick be bused daily to Hillsboro, where, isolated from the general student body population, he would spend the next six weeks in the rigid all-work, no-play environment of alternative school.

McAdams's Wolverines were shorthanded enough. Benching two late-arriving starters was out of the question.

In the mid-1980s, those traveling southbound on Interstate 35 encountered a large billboard erected by proud Abbott city fathers, boasting that their community was the birthplace of a country-and-western music icon. From the large redwood-framed sign, a larger-than-life photo of Willie Nelson, bearded and wearing his trademark red bandanna, smiled above a message that told the world that Abbott was his hometown. But no more. Legend has it that Willie had returned to town to perform at a spring evening street dance benefiting the Volunteer Fire Department, had a few more beers than usual during his performance, and eventually paid a late-night visit to the billboard. Explaining to a couple of partners in crime that the sign was "awful damn embarrassing," Nelson had doused it with five gallons of gasoline and tried to burn it down.

And although the late-night arson attempt did little more than badly singe the sign and blacken Willie's picture, a point was made. Eventually, a replacement, funded by the community's favorite son, was erected, welcoming passersby to the "Home of the Abbott High School Fighting Panthers," his old team.

For all his legendary musical success, it should be noted that back in the post–World War II '40s, when Willie was a 130-pound halfback for the Panthers, neither he nor the team had been much to brag about. It is difficult, in fact, to find anyone with specific recall of the ragtag collection of players ever winning a single game while wearing leather helmets and jerseys with numbers hand-drawn onto them. What old-timers do remember, though, about the teenaged Nelson is the picking and singing he occasionally did down at the local barbershop or as a member of the popular John Rejcek Bohemian Polka Band.

In those days, Abbott had stubbornly tried to compete against eleven-man teams from neighboring cities with far larger schools. Only when the Panthers dropped down to six-man competition had their legacy begun to grow. Now, year after year, the district championship is decided in its game against nearby Aquilla. The two teams had even coined special, though not altogether flattering, nicknames for each other. People in Abbott refer to the Aquilla players not as the Cougars, but as the "River Rats." In Aquilla, Abbott's always swift Panthers are known as the "Jackrabbits."

Randall Ballew, now anxiously returning home, had been a firsthand witness to the intense growth of the rivalry and had seen as many as two thousand fans crowd into the Abbott stadium to watch the two teams battle. He also silently wondered if there would ever come a time when Penelope football might rise to such a level.

The first thing one notices upon arriving at Panthers Stadium is that the playing field slopes noticeably from the home side to that where the visiting fans are seated. Surveyors, in fact, had once measured the decline from the southeast to northwest corners of the field at well over twenty feet. When, years earlier, it had been determined that almost forty thousand dollars worth of dirt work would be needed to correct the problem, the school board had unanimously decided it was a state of affairs the young Panthers—and their opponents—would just have to live with. And in a sense, it made the offensive strategy of the home team fairly predictable. Abbott's game plan, everyone knew, was traditionally designed to send their ball carriers running to the "downhill" side of the field.

Knowing where they would run was one thing; stopping them, another. In Ben Patrick's absence, Penelope's defense struggled. The offense, meanwhile, didn't fare much better. On the first play from scrimmage, Lozano threw a deep pass that an Abbott defender intercepted and returned for the night's first score. Then, a fumble set up another quick Panther touchdown drive. The game was but two minutes old when Abbott scored two touchdowns and kicked two conversions to take a 16–0 lead.

Penelope fans finally had something to cheer about late in the first quarter when Lozano completed a long pass to Joe Rendon and then caught a five-yard throw from Mc-Cabe for the Wolverines' first score.

And while Lozano would later score again on a seventy-five-yard kickoff return, it was clear Abbott was in control of the game. By the end of the first ten-minute quarter,

Abbott led 38–12, and its coach was already freely substituting reserves. Terry Crawford had an admirable reputation for not embarrassing opponents. Winning by the mercy rule was never his goal. Rather, he had historically made every effort to see that games lasted four quarters. On this night, it was impossible.

Though a McCabe-to-Rendon touchdown pass briefly narrowed the margin, the relentless Abbott attack never slowed. Nor did its defense. When Lozano attempted another deep pass, a Panther defender delivered a crushing blow that briefly knocked him unconscious. A Baylor University student trainer, who weekly volunteered to assist at Abbott games, examined the fallen player and suggested to the Penelope coaches that he not be allowed to continue playing. A mild concussion, he said, was a real possibility.

Helped from the field, Michael was met by his concerned father. "You OK?" Paul Lozano asked.

"Yeah," his addled son replied. "I've just got a really bad headache."

"Go sit down. I don't want you out there anymore tonight."

Minutes later, however, Michael was at McAdams's side, lobbying to return to the game. "No way," the coach said.

"Aw, come on, Coach," Lozano argued. "My dad says it's OK."

McAdams turned toward the man standing at the fence. Paul Lozano, anticipating what his son would do, was shaking his head from side to side. "Go sit down, Michael," the coach ordered.

It would soon be over anyway. With over three minutes still remaining before halftime, Abbott had built a 68–20 lead. Then, on yet another drive, they reached the Penelope one-yard line. With a forty-eight-point advantage, Coach Crawford instructed his quarterback to simply allow time to run out.

As the defeated visitors gathered around their coaches, listening as McAdams emphasized the positives of their effort ("You guys accomplished something tonight," he said. "You put twenty points on the board against one of the best teams in the state of Texas"), members of the Abbott team stood quietly by.

When the brief team meeting broke up, the Abbott team hurried toward Randall Ballew, smiling and, one by one, extending handshakes. Panthers halfback Robert Skerik, who had served as ring bearer at the Ballews' wedding, gave Randall a bear hug. So did lineman Matthew Tufts, son of his next door neighbor. "We miss you, Coach," said senior Patrick Hejl, whom Ballew often sat with during Sunday church services. Soon, the players were joined by cheerleaders, students, and several teachers who had left the stands to say hello.

Ballew's sister hugged him. "They love you," she whispered. Then, smiling, she added, "So do I."

Finally, Terry Crawford approached the Penelope coaches. "Your kids played tough," he said, "just like I expected they would. Keep after it. You guys are going to get where you want to be quicker than you think."

Leaning against one of the goalposts, Penelope superintendent Harley Johnson watched from a distance as the emotional scene played out. And he liked what he saw. Even in defeat, there had been effort and enthusiasm that he'd not seen in years past, and now, as the new season played out, a growing and well-deserved respect from those they competed against.

Normally on road trips, a quick stop at a fast-food restaurant served as the postgame meal for the players. "Tonight," Johnson told McAdams, "let's go someplace nice and buy them a steak."

━━━━━━

On other fronts, however, the Friday night atmosphere had been neither uplifting nor cause for celebration. Beyond the soft lights of the Abbotts and Penelopes, Texas high school football's dark side was making ugly headlines in the *Dallas Morning News*.

Earlier in the week in Midlothian, a few miles south of Dallas, academic failure had befallen one of the team's valued players. Several students had confronted the math

teacher who'd issued the failing mark, demanding that the player's grade be changed so that he could continue playing. The teacher, feeling threatened, had asked the students to leave her classroom. Then, when she had attempted to leave, her way was blocked.

After the teacher reported the incident to the local police, six members of the team were charged with disorderly conduct, and the matter was turned over to school administrators. Their recommendation? Two days of in-school suspension but no loss of athletic eligibility for those involved in the unfortunate incident. The failing math grade, however, went unchanged, and the player was dismissed from the team.

Meanwhile, in Everman, where the Lozanos had lived before moving to Penelope, two off-duty police officers had been surrounded and attacked by fans after a school official had asked them to remove two people who were smoking inside the stadium. Warned that the law prohibited the use of tobacco on school property, the offenders became verbally abusive, and in short order a crowd of two hundred had gathered. The officers were hit, kicked, and bitten before other police arrived to break up the brawl.

The off-duty policemen went to the emergency room. One man was arrested and charged with assaulting an officer, another with disorderly conduct.

The weekend's grand prize, however, had to go to Leonard High School. Arriving in the north Texas

community of Anna in hopes of extending an unbeaten season, the team was surprised to find deputies from the Collin County sheriff's department waiting. Immediately upon stepping from the bus, star players Lionel Bayiha and Nathan Dawson were handcuffed, read their rights, and taken to jail, charged with the assault of a young man named David Garcia in the nearby community of Blue Ridge. Garcia, according to arrest reports, had been hospitalized when hit in the head with a metal bar.

It had taken only until halftime for a Leonard fan to arrange to pay each player's fifteen-hundred-dollar bail and quickly drive the two to the stadium. In the second half, Bayiha made a key interception, caught a fifty-three-yard pass, and, with only three minutes remaining, was cheered mightily as he scored the touchdown that provided Leonard a 21–14 come-from-behind victory.

If ultimately convicted of their assault charges, Bayiha and Dawson could spend up to a year behind bars. The school's punishment? Both players were told the following Monday that they would be required to do extra running for missing the first half of the game.

13

ON WEDNESDAY EVENINGS, WHEN THE BREEZE BLOWS IN JUST the right direction and the roar of passing trucks along Farm Road 308 has quieted, those who live within Penelope's city limits can step onto their back porches and be entertained by the plaintive country ballads and toe-tapping polka music being played by the Wayward Sons Band.

Popular in Waco area tip-jar honkytonks like the Hog Creek Ice House and better-paying nightclubs as far away as Fort Worth, the band members gather weekly in David Lednicky's tool barn to have a few beers and rehearse the songs they'll perform at their weekend gigs.

On this night, however, it was neither new material nor roadhouse patrons that David was concerned about. He'd been asked to sing the National Anthem prior to the kickoff of Friday's game against Morgan and was quietly dreading it.

Standing at a microphone in a smoky dance hall, his three musical partners backing him as he picked his bass guitar and sang a medley of cheatin' and beer-drinking songs, was one thing. Doing an a cappella rendition of the National Anthem in front of friends and neighbors was something else altogether.

The thirty-eight-year-old Lednicky is a familiar face to all who attend the Penelope school, the smiling, happy-go-lucky man who daily clears away their lunchroom spills, sweeps the floors of their classrooms, and tends to myriad handyman needs. The weekend musician is also the school janitor. And for good measure, the town's elected mayor pro tem.

For years after he and wife, Debbie, married, he had driven daily to Waco, where he labored in a sheet metal shop, but when four-year-old son Derek was ready to enroll in prekindergarten, David began looking for a way to remain closer to home. Learning that the school was looking for a custodian–maintenance man–bus driver, he applied.

Though he was born in Dallas and raised in suburban Waco, it had been no great task for Debbie, an ex–Penelope High cheerleader, to persuade him to make her hometown his.

"I've never looked back," he says. "I love the small-town atmosphere and the way that people here look after each other."

And so, as the Wolverines' district meeting with Morgan neared, Lednicky steered his riding mower along the boundaries of the football field, manicuring the turf for Friday's game. As he did so, the Domesle brothers' grazing cattle lifted their heads lazily and seemed to be listening as he practiced the lyrics of the song he had agreed to sing.

———

It is not only the adults of the town who simultaneously engage in a variety of activities. As Mason Ewell hurried through the lunchroom en route to practice, Lednicky noted that the Wolverines center was sporting a black and swollen eye.

"Get that shiner in the game?" the janitor called out.

"Naw," Ewell replied. "I went to a rodeo Saturday night and entered the calf scramble. The little ol' calf didn't much like it when I finally caught him." While many of his classmates were spending their weekends strolling the mall in nearby Waco, attending movies, or hanging out at each other's homes, Mason had, for his accomplishment, earned a blue ribbon and a five-hundred-dollar gift certificate.

———

Throughout the week the coaches had shown a quiet confidence I'd not seen since the days prior to the victory against Faith Family Academy. As was their habit, they constantly insisted to the players that they had every opportunity to win; this time, however, they believed it. "I'm probably going to regret saying this," Ballew confided, "but I know damn well that we're better than they are."

Even if true, his observation hardly qualified as full-blown bragging. The Morgan High Eagles had yet to win a game. In fact, the greatest challenge its coach, Russell Hall, had faced since the school year began was keeping enough kids to field a team.

Almost weekly there had been rumors that Morgan might soon be forced to cancel the remainder of its season, forfeiting to those teams left on its schedule. Even before the season had begun, Hall had contacted each coach his team was to play, warning that if they had scheduled their Homecoming activities on the weekend his Eagles were to be the opponent, they might want to make alternative plans. At last count, he had but seven players, and either academic failure or an unexpected injury could leave them with too few to continue.

To even conduct workouts had forced the Eagles coach to take inventive measures. To keep those he had healthy, the coach rarely called for full-contact drills during the week. And instead of practicing after school, he would call his team together during a mid-day phys-ed class and enlist fellow students to demonstrate the formations and plays he expected Penelope might run.

When Hall had faxed his roster to Penelope so that it could be printed in the game program, he had listed seven players—three seniors, two juniors, and two sophomores.

However, when the visiting Eagles stepped from their team bus on Friday evening, there were only six, the minimum number required to play the game. The stepsister of senior running back David Allen had been killed in an automobile accident earlier in the week, and instead of playing football, Morgan's seventh man would be serving as a pallbearer at her funeral.

As I watched them go through their warm-up drills, I could not help but wonder at the futile battle they were fighting simply to extend a winless season. How, with not a single player in reserve, could they even consider the chance of victory? For all the struggles and shortcomings I'd witnessed in Penelope, there was obviously a place where the athletic situation was even more dire.

My sympathy was short-lived. It was quickly evident that the shorthanded visitors were lacking in neither determination nor talent.

Only minutes after David Lednicky had finished singing the National Anthem, Morgan received the opening kickoff and steadily drove toward the first touchdown of the game. Larry Garrett, filling absent teammate Allen's role, made several impressive runs, then caught a short pass for the score.

Then, on Penelope's first play from scrimmage, Lozano responded with a forty-yard burst for a touchdown. A failed extra point kick allowed Morgan to hold to an 8–6 lead.

The offensive Ping-Pong match was off and running.

It looked as if the Eagles were going to score again before Wolverine Kyle McCabe intercepted a pass at his own six-yard line to kill the drive. In the stands, Lozano's grandmother stood and cheered as Michael broke through several tackles, cut toward the sidelines, and raced seventy-four yards for his second score of the night. This time his extra point kick was good and Penelope took the lead, 14–8.

Before the opening quarter ended, he had added a thirty-five-yard touchdown run, and it appeared the game was under control. On several occasions, Morgan players had been slow to get up after being blocked or tackled, offering the reminder that the rules required each team to field six players lest officials end the game. Soon, there were even cheers from the Penelope fans as the shaken players got to their feet and play was resumed.

"These kids," said Tracy Joslin from his customary fence-line spot, "are tough." And clearly not willing to concede defeat. Morgan's Garrett and Penelope's Lozano continued to trade touchdowns throughout the second quarter. Then, as the third quarter began, Garrett scored on another long run that narrowed Penelope's lead to 30–28.

Lozano answered with a sixty-two-yard kickoff return for a touchdown. The tall and speedy Garrett responded with his fifth score of the night.

The injury that those watching had feared from the beginning came not to a Morgan player, but to Lozano. Tackled while attempting to avoid a defender, he twisted an ankle and limped to the sidelines. In his absence, Garrett continued his scoring binge, outrunning Penelope defenders for a touchdown that again narrowed the Penelope advantage to only two points.

On the sidelines, McAdams shook his head in disbelief. "If that kid doesn't make the all-district team," he told Ballew, "there's no justice."

Finally, with less than a minute remaining in the third quarter, Lozano limped back onto the field to rejoin the Penelope offense. Even with his ankle freshly taped, it was obvious he'd not likely be breaking for any more long runs. Instead, he turned passer, connecting with McCabe for a touchdown that gave his team a 41–34 advantage as the quarter ended.

With ten minutes left to play, both teams were exhausted. That the six Morgan players had fought through three quarters without rest bordered on the miraculous. The fourth quarter was barely under way when Garrett outraced the tired Wolverine defenders for another score, again closing the margin to but two points.

Ballew gathered his defense before the kickoff, all calm gone from his voice. "This," he demanded, "is where you decide whether you're going to be winners or losers. I know you're tired, but you've played too hard to let this thing slip away. We've got to stop them and get the ball back."

Which, finally, is what Penelope was able to do. On three consecutive downs, it held Morgan to short gains, forcing the first Eagles' punt of the night with only four minutes remaining in the game.

McCabe fielded the kick at midfield and looked for running room along the sideline. In front of him, Joe Rendon delivered a thundering block that lifted Morgan player Jesus Perales from his feet and sent him flying out of bounds. The cheering, however, abruptly ended when one of the referees threw a flag into the air.

Rendon's block had been well within the rules. What happened thereafter wasn't. The quick-tempered senior had stood over the fallen Perales, taunting and cursing him. Perales had jumped to his feet and grabbed Rendon's face mask. A shoving match briefly broke out until the Penelope coaches broke it up and angrily sent Rendon to the bench.

They knew what was coming. Both players were called for unsportsmanlike conduct and ejected from the game. The call left Morgan with only five eligible players.

McAdams and Ballew were quickly on the field, arguing that the officials not eject the Morgan player from the game, when Eagles coach Hall arrived to join the discussion. "Our kid was at fault," Ballew was pleading. "Eject him, but not the other guy. Let us finish the game."

Russell Hall, a tall black man with a sad, angular face, shook his head. "Can't do that," he said. "My kid was at fault, too. He knows the rules. He's out. It's over."

And so it was. With four minutes still showing on the scoreboard clock, the game had ended with Penelope a 42–40 victor. In the stands, there was only scattered cheering as fans wondered what to make of the bizarre ending.

As the two teams met for the traditional postgame handshakes, Penelope coach Bellows sought out Russell Hall. "Sir," he said, "I just want you to know how much I admire the job you're doing."

Hall smiled wearily and placed an arm around the shoulders of the young Penelope assistant. "It may wind up getting me fired," he said, "but I'm going to teach these kids that there are rules you've got to live by."

On the opposite side of the field, Ballew called Joe Rendon to his side before the team headed to the locker room. "I don't *ever* want to see or hear anything like that from you again," he said. "Never again." There was no anger in his voice. Rather, his tone was one of genuine disappointment.

It was left to McAdams to accentuate the positives. The misdeed of one player, he felt, should not be visited on the remainder of his team. And thus he left the matter of Joe Rendon's unsportsmanlike behavior to be dealt with later.

Standing amid his bone-tired players, he said, "Tonight, you guys made Penelope football history. The first two-win season. The first district victory. Be proud of yourselves." Then, reflecting on the earlier observation of his coaching father, he added, "You're going to be remembered as the Penelope team that learned how to win."

Still, there was a degree of dissatisfaction with the victory that lingered through the weekend. Inaccuracies in a small story on the game that appeared in the Saturday edition of the Waco paper didn't help. In it, the fact Morgan had played the game with only six players was highlighted. Then, it went on to report that at the time of the player ejections that prematurely ended the game, the visiting Eagles were on the verge of scoring a touchdown that would have won them the game.

"I liked it better when they didn't even bother to report our score," an angered April McAdams told her husband.

She had no problem, however, when the paper selected Morgan running back Larry Garrett as its Cen-Tex Player of the Week.

In the days that followed the Wolverines' controversial second win, I again took a respite from my fact gathering to attend to more pressing matters. The deterioration of my father's health had been further complicated when it became necessary for my mother, his daily caretaker, to enter the hospital for a long-delayed surgical procedure. Thus, instead of roaming the halls of Penelope High, I made the all-too-familiar trip back into West Texas, past the shores of Lake Brownwood, where Corey McAdams's mother, long divorced from his father, now had a home; by the Howard Payne campus, where Randall Ballew had begun his college career; and on to the little frame house on Thirteenth Street.

This time, at least, I had news of a victory to report to Dad.

Often, during late nights after he slept and I'd made a final visit to the hospital to check on Mom, I found myself thinking back on the game. Not on its long runs and back-and-forth scoring but on that midfield moment when Morgan coach Russell Hall had quietly stated the overriding purpose of his job: "I'm going to teach these kids there are rules you've got to live by."

Little did I know that on the following Friday, when, briefly relieved by a generous brother-in-law, I drove toward the community of Coolidge to attend the next-to-last game of Penelope's season, I would see firsthand the importance of Hall's coaching credo.

14

PENELOPE HIGH ENGLISH TEACHER PAULA HARLIN SAT ALONE on the visitors' side of the brightly lit Coolidge stadium, sipping at a Diet Coke as she cast a wary eye toward a bank of angry purple clouds building to the north. Her thoughts, however, were not on the imminent threat of a storm she'd heard was fast approaching, but on the scene of her late husband's greatest coaching success.

Arriving well before any other of the Wolverine supporters, she sat alone in the stands and for a few solitary minutes reminisced about this small community and how her husband had taken its Coolidge High football team to the Class A state semifinals many years ago. The town had been a bit larger then, its school still able to field an eleven-man football team, and their son Terry, Jr., had earned all-district honors as center on the team. Willie had begun elementary school there. "We had some wonderful times here," she says.

For Coolidge High, it was Homecoming night with the promise of a chilly and damp halftime coronation of the school's queen and her court. The aroma of barbecue and chili had already begun to waft from the nearby concession stand; a group of early-arriving grade school boys were on the field, tossing a scuffed football as they pretended to be members of the host Yellowjackets; and a steady stream of cars and pickups made its way into the parking lot. A small school band—unique among schools playing at the six-man level—was warming up, just as they had on those long-ago Friday nights when the Harlins had called the little farming town home. Few knew, but for Paula Harlin it was also a homecoming of sorts.

And while she sat, awaiting the arrival of the school bus that would deliver the Penelope players, a sense of bittersweet nostalgia swept over her while she remembered those days as a coach's wife. Better than anyone, she knew what McAdams, Ballew, and Bellows had dealt with during the week as they determinedly prepared their team for yet another game they had little chance to win.

No one in Penelope—not even its young coaches—had known firsthand the frustration of endless defeats the way Terry Harlin had. Before Paula's husband would finally mold teams into winners and claim district championships, and long before his crowning playoff achievement here in

Coolidge, he had made disappointing stops at a couple of small Oklahoma schools, then moved to Texas, where he coached at such out-of-the-way places as Del City, Era, Eagle Lake, and Evant. Also on his résumé was the trying agony of the Asherton High School Trojans.

———

In the early '70s, Asherton had been a migrant-worker community located deep in the cheerless wasteland of South Texas, populated by just over fifteen hundred people, whose hometown had no paved streets and boasted only a dry goods store, a feed and seed, a small grocery, and a rundown movie house that opened only on Saturday nights and showed movies in Spanish. Out on the edge of town, a couple of gas station–liquor stores vied for trade heading south toward San Antonio or Laredo.

At the aging school, which housed 123 students, twenty-four-year-old Terry Harlin had begun working as a teacher and coach of the football, basketball, and baseball teams after signing a contract that would pay him $7,200 annually. The eleven-man football program he inherited had not won a game in three years. By the end of his first season, the losing streak had extended to forty games, a negative record unmatched at the time in Texas high school football annals.

The futility was born of dirt-poor finances and grinding apathy. Harlin's teams wore hand-me-down equipment discarded and donated by nearby schools. There were no funds for a training room or a projector with which to review films of previous games. His nonexistent budget, in fact, did not allow for filming of games. Or even the traditional end-of-the-season letter jackets for those who played. There was so little interest on the part of the students that the hope of fielding a junior high team had been dismissed years earlier. Harlin had no one to scout upcoming opponents as his son now did for Penelope, or to serve as an assistant coach. He drove the team bus to out-of-town games himself. His new wife helped care for the grassless, ant-bed-infested field.

A scoreboard graced the school's rundown stadium only after neighboring Carrizo Springs had decided to replace its old one. Harlin had asked for and was given the weather-worn scoreboard and, with the help of fellow teachers, erected it at the south end of his team's home field. It was a scrounge and make-do world in which Harlin and his young wife began their careers.

Harlin had never played football, his only athletic experience coming in high school, when he had been a second baseman of modest ability at his one-room Stonewall (Oklahoma) High School. But when there were no other takers to coach an Asherton team that had not only gone winless the previous season but hadn't managed to score a single touchdown, he'd reluctantly accepted the job.

Week after fall week Harlin's outmanned teams suffered lopsided defeats from rivals like Bracketville, Natilia, and Mirando City.

And then, just weeks before the 1972 season, something remarkable took place. *Parade* magazine published a story I'd written, describing the hapless plight of Harlin and his young players. The title of the article: "The Football Team That Never Wins."

Following the publication of the story, the downtrodden Asherton football team suddenly had fans and benefactors nationwide. Mail postmarked from coast to coast began arriving at the school, offering encouragement to Harlin and his Trojans. Many of the letters were accompanied by small donations to his program. A sporting goods company delivered a blocking sled for practice, another sent along reconditioned shoulder pads and helmets. A Boston television talk show host invited Harlin to appear as his guest, and a Pennsylvania radio station adopted the Trojans, asking Harlin to call collect each Friday night with the score of the game. A Houston television station dispatched a film crew to tell its viewers the story of the struggles of the winless team.

Students at Pittsburgh Holy Innocents Grade School wrote to say they were adopting Harlin's team as their own as did the inmates of the Atlanta Federal Penitentiary. A deputy sheriff in Kansas wrote to say he'd coached before entering law enforcement and sent along his playbook with an offer to serve as a long-distance assistant. A California college graduate sent an application for an assistant coaching position, insisting all he would expect in return was room and board. On the same day, a similar application arrived from Syracuse, New York.

A member of the Brevard (North Carolina) High School Blue Devils wrote, pointing out that the team on which he played had won twenty-one of its twenty-three games in the past two years and hoping the diagrammed plays he sent might be of some help. A San Diego reader sent a check to be used to buy tickets to home games for Asherton grade school students who "would one day grow up to be proud members of the Trojans team." A woman in Jefferson City, Missouri, offering a mother's-eye view of that city's high school team, which at the time held the national winning-streak record, suggested that players at Asherton might well benefit from their hardships in their adult lives.

Without exception each letter received asked that Harlin let the sender know when he and his team scored their first victory.

It didn't take long. Halfway into that '72 season, Asherton scored a 12–6 victory over the Crystal City junior varsity, setting off a celebration unlike any the community had ever seen. On that glorious night, when the losing streak had finally ended at forty-three, a proud Paula Harlin had tearfully watched as her husband was carried off the field on the shoulders of his players.

In her English class, she recalls, students were assigned the happy duty of writing letters that spread the good news to such far-flung places as Hanford, California; Fairfax, Indiana; and Peaks Island, Maine.

By season's end the Trojans had added three more victories. Local fans had even broken their stay-at-home tradition and begun following the team to out-of-town games. A renewed spirit surged through the student body as the reminders of endless defeats faded, replaced by optimism and enthusiasm. In time, there would be winning seasons, even district championships. And as is traditional in the migrant world of coaching, the opportunities to move on, to revitalize other programs at other schools, came. Coach Harlin and his wife left Asherton for new challenges, leaving behind a winning program and a proud legacy.

"Terry did the same thing in Asherton that our coaches are now doing here," Harlin said as she watched Coach Ballew steer the yellow school bus carrying the Penelope squad into the stadium. "My husband made the game fun for the kids; made them believe in themselves. When those kids recognized the fact there was someone who really cared about them, they worked really hard at getting better. And finally, they began to win."

It is a slow transition she has quietly watched during the short time since the Wolverines started up their program again.

———

Earlier in the day, while the coaches stood on the practice field, watching as the junior high players hurried to the dressing room for a quick after-practice shower before making their way to the cafeteria, talk turned to the varsity's evening trip to Coolidge.

"It won't take us more than thirty minutes to get there," Ballew said. "Why don't we let the kids get dressed and taped and do their pregame warm-ups right here before we leave? Let the Coolidge kids wonder where we are right up until a few minutes before time for kickoff. Who knows? It might just distract them a little."

McAdams, aware that once more his team was the underdog pick on Granger Huntress's Web site, smiled. "At this point," he acknowledged, "I'll try anything. If the bus doesn't break down, maybe it'll give us a little edge."

In truth, both knew, the Coolidge players, although far more talented than Penelope's, had a reputation for being disorganized and undisciplined. Their coach, Stephen Gunter, was the fourth the school had hired in as many years. And though he was making headway as he worked to provide stability and direction to the program, frustrating problems remained. Several of his players routinely skipped practices without valid excuses. Penalties for un-sportsmanlike behavior were commonplace during games. And lack of proper attention to academics was an ongoing problem.

Ballew, in fact, had applied for the Coolidge coaching position a few years earlier and had been interviewed twice before the job was given to another applicant. In retro-spect, he admits, it might have been a blessing in disguise.

Still, if the Coolidge players had been concerned about the visitors' late arrival, it didn't show. They needed only two of-fensive plays to score their first touchdown. As the first quarter wound down, the bigger and faster Yellowjackets, featuring a freshman running back with the unlikely name of Romeo Brown, had built a 22–0 lead, and rumblings began among the Penelope fans that they would be making early departures for home. "This one," said Paul Lozano, "is gonna be over at halftime." The dreaded forty-five-point rule again loomed as a real possibility. Only a seventy-yard kickoff return for a touchdown by his son in the fading sec-onds of the opening quarter and a ten-yard burst into the end zone after teammate Josh Hampton had intercepted a Coolidge pass ensured that the game would continue into the second half.

The score had widened to 40–14 when center Mason Ewell suffered a dislocated shoulder. As he lay on the field, being attended to by the coaches, his mother and stepfather joined the midfield huddle around the injured youngster. By the time the Homecoming Queen candidates began gathering on the opposite side of the field, eager for their moment in the halftime spotlight, a grim-faced Michelle Joslin was backing her SUV from its parking spot to drive her son to the hospital.

Among those standing by the car to wish the injured player well were a young couple from the Dallas area attending their third Penelope game of the season. Computer programmer Bill Good and wife Tina had a weekend habit of prowling the Texas back roads on idle weekends and had happened onto Penelope during one leisurely Sunday drive. The vacant downtown buildings raised myriad questions about what the community had once been and why it had died away to nothing but the post office and the nearby school. On numerous business trips to Waco, the thirty-four-year-old Bill Good, raised in the big-city bustle, found himself making side trips to Penelope. He searched the Internet for historical information and lingered in the post office, listening as Mary Dvorak told stories that had been handed down to her and viewing her collection of faded photos of the town in its heyday.

In time, the Goods began setting aside their Friday evenings to attend the Wolverines football games, where they became acquainted with local residents. "I really can't explain the fascination," Bill admits, "but there is a warm and comforting feeling here. We can come here, and for a few hours the troubles of the world disappear."

The immediate plight of the Penelope players, however, remained. Although they did manage to avoid an early end to the game, Coolidge had continued to score almost at will throughout the second half. The final score: 74–26.

As McAdams gathered his team at midfield, he had little to say. The players, he knew, were weary, tired of defeat and the daily practices that had been under way since August. "Forget this one," he finally said. "Start thinking about what we need to do to get better before our last game. *Our last game*. You seniors will soon be playing the final football game of your life. Start thinking about making it your best."

Mike Lozano only stared at the turf as his coach spoke.

When his teammates began walking toward the bus, the young running back sought out his father, who was still standing near the visitors' stands. "What's the matter?" Paul asked as his son approached.

"I'm not playing next week," Michael said. "I'm through."

"Why?"

"Nobody was even trying to block. I can't run the ball if nobody . . . "

"Hey," Paul Lozano said, cutting off his discouraged son's observation, "don't do something you'll regret for the rest of your life. You're tired and disappointed. If you've really got a problem, talk to the coach about it, not me." His voice was controlled, little more than a whisper. He knew the highly competitive nature of his son and admired it. He also knew that there were those on the team who did not share the same intensity, that over the course of the season a resentment had steadily grown among some of the players over Michael's "star" status.

The young Lozano's frustration, however, was slight compared to that of a Coolidge player who came walking toward the field, shoulder pads in one hand, helmet in the other. As a bus passed, taking his teammates across town to the school, the youngster began screaming curses. Coach Gunter, who was still on the field, talking with the Penelope coaches, walked quickly to the fence near where the angered teenager was standing.

"What are you doing?"

The player pointed to the disappearing bus and called out the assistant coach's name. "He threw me off. Said he didn't like my attitude and I could walk." With that he angrily hurled his helmet onto the middle of the field.

The Coolidge coach said nothing as the young player's rant continued.

Nearby, a stunned Mike Lozano watched the bizarre tirade as discussion of his own frustrations abruptly ended. An outburst like that, he knew, would quickly curtail the playing days of anyone on the Penelope team. His coaches would never tolerate such behavior.

His father pointed in the direction of the Coolidge player. "That," Paul Lozano told his son, "is a perfect example of what you're never going to be. Understand what I'm saying?"

Michael grinned at his father, nodded, then jogged away to join his teammates.

As the team began the trip home, the offhand remark made earlier in the day by McAdams became prophecy. Just before the Penelope school bus reached the outskirts of Hubbard, driver Ballew noticed the red light on the temperature gauge blinking. The engine's fan belt had broken. Slowing to a crawl, he managed to make it to the lone open service station–convenience store in town, and while tired and disgruntled players piled out to buy soft drinks, chips, and candy bars, the assistant coach was persuading a passerby to give him a ride to Penelope, where he could get another school bus to transport the team home.

It was past midnight and raining when the tired and aching players filed into the locker room to shed their uniforms. At the hospital in nearby Hillsboro, an emergency room doctor had reset Mason Ewell's dislocated shoulder and placed his arm in a protective sling. Directing his attention to Mason's mother, the doctor advised that her son wear the sling for at least three weeks.

Tears welled in Mason's eyes, not because of the pain but from disappointment that he might not be able to play in the season's final game alongside his best friend, Kyle McCabe.

15

ENELOPE, TEXAS, IS NOT WITHOUT ITS IMPERFECTIONS. ONE
evening, as Mike Baker and I lingered over a chicken-
fried steak, I asked what he felt its greatest shortcoming
was, what might, in his opinion, be most lacking in the social and educational growth of its children.

His answer came quickly: "Diversity." It was a word of
concern I'd heard often from his fellow teachers and school
administrators, even from some of its more introspective
students. Collectively, they expressed worry that the racial
isolation of their community might make the transition to
adult life difficult for those who would one day venture beyond the invisible boundaries of their upbringing.

For years there had not been a single African-American student enrolled in the Penelope school system, not
one black residing within the city limits. Now, fifth-grader

Anjali West and her older sister, Kenyedra, a freshman, accounted for the 1.7 percent of black students attending classes.

The racial makeup of McAdams's football team adds emphasis to the shortfall: nine Anglo players, five Hispanics, no blacks.

Historically and predominantly white and Czech, the small enrollment had expanded in recent years to include an increasing number of Hispanic students, whose parents had come seeking farmhand jobs and the uncomplicated benefits of rural living. But why so few African-Americans? Why did the black teenagers who were daily driven from nearby Malone to continue their high school education choose Bynum instead of Penelope?

Lack of adequate housing and a severely limited job market for their parents were and continue to be a significant roadblock. And trivial though it might sound, football—or, more specifically, the longtime lack of it—had been another of the myriad and complicated reasons. For years the absence of the sport in Penelope had made the choice easy for many young Malone males, black and white. If they wanted to play high school football, enrolling at Penelope, which didn't have a program, wasn't an option. And so it had become traditional for them to climb aboard school buses that took them eight miles north to Bynum High School. In time, their annual migration became based more on family tradition than on any concern they would be unwelcome in Penelope. If Mom and Dad had attended school in Bynum, so did their kids. And their kids' friends and neighbors.

In this part of the world, where tradition carries high value, such habits are difficult to break. Those who whispered that Penelope might be antiblack, its people racist, based their opinion only on the demographic makeup, not the town's attitude. Was the word *nigger* occasionally spoken in Penelope? Unfortunately, yes. But when it was, it generally came from the mouths of a few of the community's old-timers. The same can be said of every city and town, regardless of how open-minded and forward-thinking, that I've visited during a lifetime roaming the South and elsewhere.

"When Edward West came to me several years ago to talk about enrolling his girls here," superintendent Johnson remembers, "we had no African-American students. He didn't beat around the bush. He'd heard that we had a good school but wanted to know if his children were likely to encounter racial problems. All I could do was assure him that I didn't foresee it."

Today, West and his wife, Chanel, are pleased with the education their children are receiving. Anjali, who has attended the Penelope school since kindergarten and is now a student in April McAdams's fifth-grade class, is popular with her classmates and a regular winner in math and spelling at UIL competitions. Big sister Kenyedra is an honor roll student and a promising member of Coach Kreder's volleyball team.

And now, there is every indication that additional African-American students will soon join the West children. Since it was decreed last year that Penelope would be the primary "receiving school" of high-school-bound Malone students, a bus daily visited the campus during the fall, bringing with it seventh- and eighth-graders to practice with the junior high football team. With three black members on the team, it was on its way to a three-way tie for the district championship. And the visiting youths were collectively talking of the day they would become members of the Wolverines team.

It is, in fact, some of those young players who give Corey McAdams reason to be optimistic about the future of his program. And give Johnson reason to see a more diverse enrollment on the horizon.

"Once we get a few more African-American families to enroll their children here," Johnson says, "they'll see what we have to offer. When they do, I'm convinced others will follow."

And, he adds, the Penelope school system will be better for it.

Since the Wolverines had arrived at an open date on their schedule, leaving the final game of the season two weeks away, I seized the opportunity to explore the picturesque back roads of the region. On one late afternoon, I idly drove the streets of Abbott in search of Willie Nelson's boyhood home, on another I had, for no good reason, made the thirty-mile drive to Mexia, where former *Playboy* playmate and pop culture celebrity Anna Nichole Smith had grown up and worked at the local Dairy Queen. In Hubbard, I visited the cemetery where baseball legend Tris Speaker is buried. And I traveled to West to resample what I already knew to be the best Czech pastries made this side of Prague.

And then, as I wound along Farm Road 744, I happened on an ethnic irony I'd never read about in my own youthful exposure to Texas history. Just six miles east of Malone, I arrived in the fading hamlet of Pelham, Texas, the only all-black community in the entire state. Such, I soon learned, had been the case since the town had been established by freed slaves in 1866.

Whereas Penelope, just twenty miles away, might have been home to only a few blacks during its lengthy history, Pelham had, since the final shots of the Civil War, never known a white resident.

Originally called Folks on the Creek, changed to Pelham by a homesick postmaster's wife who wished that it be renamed after her Alabama hometown, the town had once flourished. On the two hundred acres former slave owners allotted each slave family, cotton and corn had been planted and harvested. Businesses opened, churches were built, and children attended the Pelham School. At the height of the town's prosperity, the population had reached 350.

That's how lifetime residents Darlene Holloway and Elayne Robinson, women whose scholastic careers had been completed long before integration became part of the national landscape, remember it. They had attended Pelham's school, then taught there as others followed. But ultimately, like other all-black public schools in Texas, it had closed, its students being sent off to share classrooms with white students in nearby Hubbard.

Today, there are no children among the twenty-five or so remaining residents. Pelham has no future, only a past.

On the day of my visit I found Holloway and Robinson at the old two-story schoolhouse, where they regularly serve as volunteer caretakers of the town's history. Today, the whitewashed frame building serves as the Pelham Community History Museum, filled with old photographs, artifacts, and carefully collected oral histories that recall times when the townspeople worked and played, danced on Saturday nights, and listened to fire-and-brimstone sermons on Sunday mornings, and when the Pelham High basketball team won the collection of time-worn trophies still proudly on display in the museum.

It had been a different time, they suggested while guiding my mid-afternoon tour. In the long ago days of their youth, Pelham had been a happy and comfortable place to live. They could no more have imagined a white family moving into their little town than Penelope pioneers could have foreseen the day when the need for diversity would be a valid issue among their townspeople.

Which is to say that racial issues have a long, tattered, and immeasurably complex history along the hidden back roads of my homeland. More close in age to the museum keepers in Pelham than to many of those I'd come to know in Penelope, I've seen the dark and ugly struggles of the Civil Rights Movement, watched the "whites only" signs grudgingly removed from public places, heard the hateful rhetoric of Klan diehards, and listened to painful recollections of survivors of the infamous bombing of a black Birmingham, Alabama, church that claimed the lives of four innocent children. I've heard the language evolve from *Negro* and *colored* to *black* and *African-American,* and I've felt the long-overdue embarrassment at the misguided notion that simply because I had the good fortune to be born white I had somehow earned greater entitlement.

And I'm convinced that things are better now. There is no longer need for the isolated safety of a Pelham, hidden away from the threats of injustice and violence spawned by nothing more than the color of one's skin. Nor is there reason for a few shadowy and stubborn Penelope residents to fear that their community might somehow be endangered by the arrival of new people, new ideas, and new thinking.

"We'll get there," Johnson promises. It is, he freely admits, the last unfulfilled goal of his career as an educator.

———————

The immediate goal of the Penelope coaches during the last week in October was to keep their players focused on a final game of the season that was still fourteen days in the future. Although contending teams always looked forward to an open week on their schedule as a welcome breather, a time to allow nagging injuries to heal and tired legs to be rested, for the Wolverines it was little more than a delay of the inevitable. With no chance to advance into the playoffs, no possibility of a winning record, the general feeling was that they would like to get it over with as soon as possible. The enthusiasm, if not completely gone, had at least seriously waned.

Even the coaches were having difficulty hiding the toll taken by the long season. Where once the door to their tiny office was forever open prior to practices, it was now closed. Behind it, McAdams, Ballew, and Bellows sat, often in silence, none wishing to be the first to admit the dread of another day's workout.

In truth, the players were feeling no better. With Mason Ewell's injured shoulder preventing him from workouts and Ben Patrick scholastically ineligible, the team was already seriously depleted when Joe Rendon, the Wolverines' leading receiver, began skipping practices. At first, he had offered a variety of lame excuses when confronted by the coaches. By week's end, however, it had become clear that once more he would not finish a season he had begun. In the hallways, he avoided making eye contact with coaches and teammates.

"He's gone," McAdams finally said to his assistants. Why? "Beats me. He won't say." And what to do about it? McAdams decided that rather than officially dismiss him from the team, he would simply say and do nothing. The decision not to participate in the final days of the season, to turn his back on teammates he had labored with since those first hot August afternoon practices, would be the player's burden to bear.

"He's going to regret it," Ballew suggested.

"That," McAdams acknowledged, "might be a good thing for him."

Even Michael Lozano's anticipation of the final game, in which he had the opportunity to complete his season as the district's leading rusher, was muted. Each evening, once football practice ended, he hurried home to shoot baskets at the portable backboard in front of his home. Instead of the upcoming game against Kopperl, he was already looking ahead to the basketball season.

Most concerned by the lack of enthusiasm, it seemed, was Kyle McCabe. An intense competitor, the senior co-captain not only barked encouragement to his weary teammates, daily reminding them that finishing out the season with their best effort was essential, but spent his evenings at the Joslin home, urging best friend Mason Ewell to plan to suit up for their last game as teammates. "I want you on the field," McCabe said, "but if you can't, I at least want you in your uniform, standing with me on the sidelines."

Even though his parents were discouraging such thoughts, Mason had secretly planned to play. And just days before the scheduled game, he knocked on the door of the coach's office, a note from his doctor in hand. "I'm good to go," he announced. In the hallway behind him, Kyle stood, smiling for the first time in days.

Theirs is, at best, a strange-looking partnership.

Mason Ewell is the kid you remember from your own school days, the one always certain to be voted Most Friendly Boy. Quick to smile and greet classmates with a pat on the back, he is, at sixteen, still in the process of shedding the baby fat from his five foot six, 180-pound frame. Kyle, meanwhile, is rail thin, built more like a basketball forward than a quarterback, and a head taller than his friend. Quieter, more reserved—an admitted worrier—there are days when he smiles rarely, if at all.

They had met soon after Mason's parents, Tracy and Michelle Joslin, had purchased their four-hundred-acre cattle ranch north of town. Wearied by the hectic pace and rising crime statistics in suburban Dallas, they had gone in search of a rural environment in which to raise Michelle's two sons. In 1999, they made the move to Penelope.

By the time their oldest, Morgan, graduated in the class of 2004, the Joslins were fully welcomed members of the community. Michelle served as booster club president for the school's Future Farmers of America chapter and volunteered in the concession stand at football and basketball games. Tracy had been a friendly and familiar face at sporting events, home and away, since Morgan had been part of the inaugural Wolverine football team.

And for all practical purposes, the Joslins had inherited a third son. Kyle, who had been the first to greet and befriend young Mason and introduce him to his future classmates, was soon spending as much time in their home as he did in his own. Since junior high, the two had been inseparable.

It was, in many ways, an attraction of opposites: Mason enjoyed a strong and supportive relationship with his mother and stepdad as well as with his biological father, who regularly drove to Penelope to watch him play. Tall and bony, Kyle had a family history that was less idyllic. He'd never known his father, who had left just days after he was born. And while his permanent address was a small house on the outskirts of nearby Birone, where his mother, Linda, and truck-driving stepfather, Robert Turner, lived, he never invited friends there and rarely spoke of his parents to teachers or classmates. Instead, his life generally revolved around the Joslin house and the athletic field, where Coach McAdams not only schooled him in passing techniques but lent his own quiet support. "You're not supposed to have favorites," McAdams once admitted to me, "but the truth is, Kyle's special to me. And it has nothing to do with his athletic ability. He's overcome a lot to make himself what he is."

It had not gone unnoticed that neither of McCabe's parents had attended a Wolverines game.

During the previous summer months, in fact, Kyle had lived at the Joslin home while working as a carpenter's assistant to Tracy Joslin, visiting his own parents only occasionally. When, a year earlier, there had been rumors that he might soon move to Temple to live with his grandmother, Michelle Joslin had quietly assured him he would be welcome to live with them. Since then, friends in search of Kyle always first dialed the number at the Joslin house. When time came to shop for new school clothes, it was Michelle who accompanied him. Her husband, meanwhile, had helped him buy a used car with his summer earnings.

While stadium lights lit the Friday night skies in surrounding communities, the people of Penelope briefly dismissed the struggles of their Wolverines and, instead, hurried toward the elementary school gymnasium for the annual Fall

Festival activities. Giddy children held to parents' hands as they arrived in their Halloween best, eager to play games and sample the trick-or-treat sweets that waited. Teachers and high school students manned booths inside. Outside, a hayride waited. As I wandered through the festive atmosphere, it occurred to me that the population of the community must have magically doubled with the sweep of some witch's wand.

"There are people here from all over the county," April McAdams shouted above the noise as she pointed toward her husband. All teachers, she explained, were mandated to help with the fund-raising carnival. Superintendent Johnson, however, had agreed that the football coaches could be granted early leave so they might drive over to Kopperl and scout their upcoming opponent.

Later that evening, as I sat with them among the crowd on hand for the Kopperl-Coolidge game, I easily recognized the reason they were anxious about the following week's game. Kopperl was pounding the team that had easily defeated Penelope the week before—so badly, in fact, that the forty-five-point rule would end the game soon after the Penelope coaches' arrival.

Following the game, the Penelope coaches remained until the victory celebration had quieted, then sought out Kopperl coach Gary Harkins to offer their congratulations. "We'll see you guys next week," McAdams said. "Be kind," a smiling Ballew whispered.

And with that the assistant coach turned and quickly began walking in the direction of the darkened baseball field. "I'll meet you at the car," he told McAdams. "I want to check something out."

Minutes later he was back, a broad grin on his face. "There are big ol' deer tracks all over the infield," he said. "Hunting's going to be good this year." His thoughts, too, had begun to drift toward things other than football.

16

O N THE FIRST TUESDAY MORNING IN NOVEMBER, THE USUALLY deserted downtown of Penelope was abuzz with activity. Pickups lined both sides of the street as residents hurried through a gentle rain in the direction of the Volunteer Fire Department. It was Election Day, and people were arriving in force to make their voices heard.

On the streets and inside the building, however, there was little argument over whether incumbent George W. Bush or his Democratic challenger, John Kerry, should spend the next four years in the White House, and none of the venomous political rhetoric that had, for months, poisoned the radio talk shows and editorial pages. In Penelope, there were greater concerns:

Would Sam McClendon, running for county commissioner, keep his campaign promise and finally get something done about their rain-rutted farm roads? Which of the candidates for county sheriff, Brent Button or Clark Grindstaff, was most likely to see to it that no more clandestine methamphetamine labs sprang into operation out in the dark corners of the county? And if elected, would Mariel Eubank serve as a fair and honest tax assessor?

It was not politics, however, that concerned Johnson on the day of the final game. Rather, it was custodian David Lednicky's discovery of a trail of holes pitted along one end of the football field. The Domesle brothers' cows had, during the night, managed to break through the fence and find better grazing inside the freshly mown stadium. As Johnson worried aloud that someone might be injured despite the repair work Lednicky had already done, I was reminded of an old West Texas football tale I'd heard years earlier.

"Ever heard of Cow Patty Bingo?" I asked the superintendent.

Pleased that he hadn't, I proceeded:

As the story goes, the coach of a small, dirt-poor farming community school had wracked his brain for some way to raise badly needed funds for his football program. In desperation—and with a little help from a local dairy owner—he had devised a game of chance that he was certain would bring the needed money into the coffers.

Lining the football field into a massive checkerboard design and numbering each of the hundreds of squares, he then set about selling chances at a dollar per square. Then, when all the squares had been purchased, a cow was set loose on the field, free to roam and graze and, well, tend to the bodily function farm animals frequently tend to.

When the results of nature's call landed on one of the purchased squares, some happy winner would claim fifty dollars. The remainder of the money collected would be used to purchase badly needed equipment.

Johnson laughed. Penelope's economic situation, he assured me, wasn't likely to ever get *that* desperate.

———

As I arrived for the last home game of the season, I saw Joe Rendon standing near the concession stand, looking in my direction. Although his construction worker stepfather was the only man in Penelope who wore his hair in a shoulder-length ponytail, Rendon adhered to the close-cut style favored by his classmates. Muscular and broad-shouldered, he, like Lozano, had the easy, confident look of an athlete. "Line up every boy in school against a wall and ask someone to pick out the one who looks like he'd be the best player in the bunch," says McAdams, "and they'd probably select Joe."

Yet he was not in uniform.

Smiling sheepishly, he knew what I would ask: "Why aren't you playing tonight?"

Hands stuffed deep into his jeans, the broad-shouldered teen only shrugged. "Aw, I just screwed up," he finally replied. Then, looking out toward the field where his former teammates were going through pregame drills, he added, "I wish I was."

I could have pressed harder for an explanation, but as I'd learned in my days as a parent, trying to make good sense of teenage reason is often a fruitless undertaking. I'd heard the rumors: That he and Michael had been arguing over the fact he was dating Michael's younger sister, Tiffani. And although apparently true, the disagreement served as no legitimate reason in light of the fact that Lozano had been among those who had urged him to return to the team. I'd also heard that he'd simply never wanted to play football in the first place and had, in a rebellious moment, made a snap decision to walk away. Once his mistake was made, he had been unable to fashion any graceful, face-saving way to seek reinstatement.

Whatever the reason, Rendon and his parents would be denied one of the most memorable moments of the season. Traditionally, the final home game is designated Senior Night. Each player in his last year of football escorts his parents onto the field at halftime for a final salute from the fans.

On this night, instead of three, there would be only two seniors honored: Lozano and McCabe.

And in the days leading up to the game, there had been whispered concern that Kyle McCabe might be standing alone. McAdams had avoided asking his quarterback if his parents were planning to attend and, instead, had written them a letter, informing them of the planned event and inviting their participation.

It was while he stood on the edge of the playing field, watching his team go through pregame drills, that the Wolverines coach had turned to see a tanned and lanky man approaching, his hand extended. "Hope you boys get 'em tonight," he said. For another minute or two they exchanged small talk, then the man turned and disappeared into the arriving crowd.

McAdams could not place the well-wisher—until, looking out toward his team, he saw Kyle steal a glance in his direction. Only then did the coach realize that he had, for the first time, met his quarterback's stepfather.

There was a genuine sense of relief that seemed to sweep through the entire stadium as Kyle's parents arrived shortly before kickoff and made their way into the stands.

Briefly, it appeared that the game they would see might serve as a fitting completion of their son's football career. After Kopperl took a 6–0 lead midway through the opening quarter, Kyle directed the team downfield effortlessly, then threw a twenty-yard touchdown pass to Lozano to tie the score.

Then, however, the visitors' offense kicked into high gear. Eagles running back Jason Williams, leading Lozano in the race for the district rushing title, sped through the depleted Wolverines defense almost at will.

By halftime, Penelope trailed 34–6. Despite McAdams's locker room exhortations, it was obvious the season was over. It became official just three minutes into the third period when the Kopperl advantage climbed to 55–6 and officials ended the game.

Players huddled as Randall Ballew gave his final postgame prayer of the season, then wandered idly among parents and classmates who had come onto the field. Sophomore Josh Hampton, most likely the heir to Lozano's starting duties at running back next season, sought out announcer Mike Baker to thank him for calling his name over the public address system. Cheerleaders gathered their megaphones for a final time. As if not quite ready to grasp the fact the season was suddenly over, fans were slower than usual to make their way to the parking lot.

I briefly searched the crowd for Kyle McCabe's parents before Paul Lozano told me they had already left.

During the three months that had evolved from the hundred-degree practice days of August to this crisp November evening, the Wolverines and the people of Penelope had experienced only minor differences in their lives. A couple of games had been won, giving rise to short-lived celebration and optimism for the seasons to come; a new Homecoming Queen had been crowned; and the stands had been filled every Friday night. In ways they probably didn't even recognize, coaches McAdams, Ballew, and Bellows had positively affected the life of the community.

In truth, however, little of significance had really changed. And therein I found the beauty.

POSTSCRIPT

And now it is a late December afternoon, and a clear-day sunset is casting shadows on the empty Penelope football field. School has been dismissed for the long-awaited Christmas break, and the only sign of life is a slow-moving tractor on the far horizon, lending proof that although all about him might stop to rest, a farmer's work is never done. The once-verdant field has turned straw-colored, and as I stand there, a gentle wind blowing, I understand something Superintendent Johnson once confided to me. At the end of workdays that have, for whatever reason, been particularly demanding, he occasionally slips from his office to come here for a few minutes of solitude in what he judges the most peaceful and scenic spot in town.

The season, and my journey, have ended. Now the students and townspeople have turned their thoughts to midterm exams, basketball, and the fast-approaching holidays. Though darkness is still a while away, gaily-colored lights already twinkle from the eaves and rooftops of several houses. And as with the constant flow of all things, there have been changes, large and small, since my last visit.

I sat at my comatose father's side, telling him things he was unable to hear, as he peacefully passed away only weeks after his last football season ended prematurely.

We never got to discuss the fact that while the 2–8 Wolverines I'd become so fond of played out their season in the shadows, ranked only ninety-eighth in Granger Huntress's final six-man poll, other Texas high schools had basked in the national spotlight. The Southlake Carroll Dragons had done their multi-million-dollar stadium proud, going 16–0 en route not only to the state Class AAAAA eleven-man championship but to the number-one spot in the national schoolboy rankings kept by *USA Today* and the National Prep Poll. Their coach, Todd Dodge, was honored as the country's top high school coach. And in his final press conference of the year, recently reelected President Bush had praised the Crawford High Pirates on national television, noting that the team from his Texas home had captured the Class AA state title.

In Penelope, Kyle McCabe, after making it through the football season without injury, had seriously damaged a knee in the early stages of the basketball season and was all but resigned to dismissing a future athletic career at the collegiate level. On the good news side of things, he received honorable mention on the Waco paper's Super Centex All-Academic team.

Meanwhile, Mike Lozano, having again been named to the all-district team, was talking more and more about higher education. Maybe, he'd begun telling his father, he would one day become a high school football coach and history teacher, a clear sign that he'd adopted Randall Ballew as a role model. Though still a self-assured young man, he remains painfully naive about the world outside. One day as we talked of his future, he asked if I knew of any colleges where they play six-man football. Ben Patrick, his alternative-school sentence completed, was back in the mainstream and faring better, both socially and academically, eagerly talking of reporting for football again next fall. Still, though, he refers to Mississippi as home and longs for the day when he can return there. One day, he says, he hopes to make a career of law enforcement. Joe Rendon, still quick-tempered, had been told he could attend no more sporting events for the remainder of the school year after becoming involved in an altercation at a basketball game in nearby Bynum. As the Wolverines had been on their way to defeating their archrival, a scuffle had broken out on the court when a Bynum player had grabbed and shoved Lozano. Rendon, a spectator, had left the stands to join in the brief fray. No real harm had been done; still, Johnson had decided, harsh discipline was called for.

All in all, however, the gentle flow of this rural American town continues. Gloria Walton is still agonizing over what one-act play her student actors will perform in the spring, and Paula Harlin and April McAdams are busy prepping those who will participate in writing, debate, and poetry reading at the upcoming district UIL competition. Penelope grad Jason Atkins continues to serve in Iraq, though now more removed from harm's way than he was earlier. In that knowledge, Veda Atkins now sleeps a bit better. Lauren Watson is still sending Jason e-mails and letters to keep him updated on happenings back home. David Lednicky and his Wayward Sons are busier than ever, performing at various Waco nightspots almost every weekend. He is planning to start giving Ben Patrick, whom he's come to like during their daily bus trips to alternative school, guitar lessons.

And it has not taken long for the coaches to begin talk of next year's season. Royce McAdams lent his son a surprise hand recently when he arrived with a pickup-load of weight-lifting equipment that was no longer being used at his Little River Academy. For the first time, the Wolverines coaches will be able to conduct a serious off-season strength program. With most of the team returning and the addition of new players from the championship junior high team, they are optimistic. They are even hearing rumors that several high school students who didn't play during the fall are now talking of joining the team in 2005.

Theirs is an optimism I find both contagious and uplifting. In the Penelopes of the world, life goes on, not without its bumps and bruises, but always in the sane and simple belief that good times will forever trump the bad, that the next victory is always waiting on the horizon.

My visit confirmed that there remains in our society the basic good upon which we've historically flourished. Though but a faint star in the multitude, Penelope is the proof I had come to find. Its people are a composite of the clichés too often mocked: hard-working and God-fearing; rising above the two-dollar, rush-to-the-bank-on-payday woes, to embrace the day and extend a helping hand. Seventeen-year-old Audra Osborne, perhaps, described it best: "You might get a call some night from a friend who is looking for materials needed to complete a project for school the next day. It will turn out that it isn't *that* person who needs them, but someone who called them. It will continue along the chain until whatever is needed is found. By the time it's over, you might not even know who it is you're helping. That's how we do things here."

In Penelope, Texas, I learned, the chief currency is a simple act of kindness.

That's what its people—coaches and students, administrators and teachers, moms and dads—offered to me. And for that I thank them one and all.

2004
PENELOPE HIGH
SCHOOL WOLVERINES

Kyle McCabe	Senior	QB/FS	6'0"	170
Joe Rendon	Senior	E/LB	5'10"	170
Michael Lozano	Senior	RB/FS	5'6"	150
Mason Ewell	Junior	C/DE	5'6"	180
Tyler Beasley	Junior	E/CB	5'8"	150
Josh Hampton	Sophomore	RB/CB	5'5"	130
Kevin Altamirano	Sophomore	RB/DE	5'8"	145
Josh Young	Sophomore	E/DE	5'8"	215
Javier Marin	Sophomore	E/LB	5'7"	165
Ben Patrick	Sophomore	RB/DE	6'0"	155
Jonathan Moreno	Freshman	E/DE	6'0"	160
Chris Culpepper	Freshman	E/DE	5'8"	160
Ethan Osborne	Freshman	E/DE	5'8"	165
Chad Kerr	Freshman	RB/CB	6'0"	160

Coaches: Corey McAdams, Randall Ballew, Charles Bellows

ABOUT THE AUTHOR

Carlton Stowers has twice received the Mystery Writers of America's Edgar Allen Poe Award for the year's Best Fact Crime Book and has also won the Violet Crown Award for Texas's Best Book of Non-Fiction. Stowers is also the recipient of numerous awards for his newspaper and magazine work, and his *Dallas Observer* story on Penelope and its football team was anthologized in 2004's *Best American Sports Writing*. He lives outside of Dallas.